THE ULTIMATE
GUITAR
CHRISTMAS
FAKE BOOK

ISBN 0-634-01818-3

HAL•LEONARD®
CORPORATION
7777 W. BLUEMOUND RD. P.O. BOX 13819 MILWAUKEE, WI 53213

Visit Hal Leonard Online at
www.halleonard.com

THE ULTIMATE GUITAR CHRISTMAS FAKE BOOK

CONTENTS

STRUM AND PICK PATTERNS

This chart contains the suggested strum and pick patterns that are referred to by number at the beginning of each song in this book. The symbols ⊓ and ∨ in the strum patterns refer to down and up strokes, respectively. The letters in the pick patterns indicate which right-hand fingers plays which strings.

p = **thumb**
i = **index finger**
m = **middle finger**
a = **ring finger**

For example; Pick Pattern 2
is played: thumb - index - middle - ring

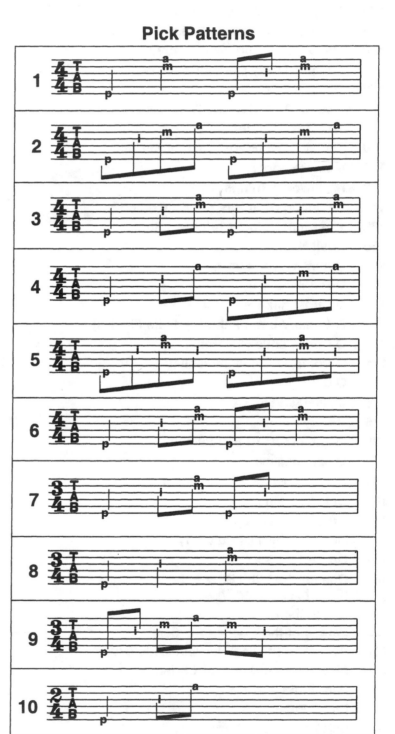

Strum Patterns   **Pick Patterns**

You can use the 3/4 Strum or Pick Patterns in songs written in compound meter (6/8, 9/8, 12/8, etc.).
For example, you can accompany a song in 6/8 by playing the 3/4 pattern twice in each measure.
The 4/4 Strum and Pick Patterns can be used for songs written in cut time (¢) by doubling the note time values in the patterns. Each pattern would therefore last two measures in cut time.

A Caroling We Go

Music and Lyrics by Johnny Marks

Strum Pattern: 8
Pick Pattern: 8

Verse

Moderately Bright

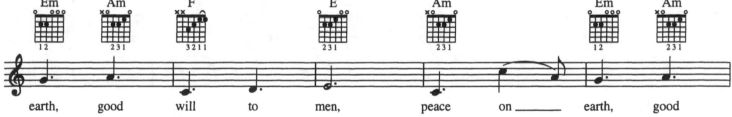

1. A (4.) car - ol - ing, a car - ol - ing, a car - ol - ing we go,
2., 3. *See Additional Lyrics*

hearts filled with mu - sic and cheeks a - glow. _____ From

Chorus

house to house we bring the mes - sage of the King a - gain: Peace on _____

earth, good will to men, peace on _____ earth, good

1., 2., 3. will to men. _____

4. 2. We men. _____
4. A -

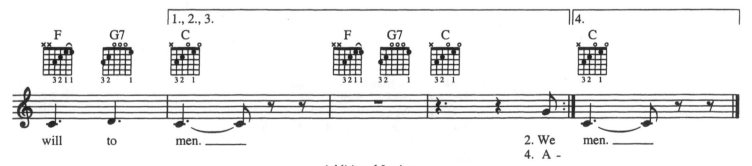

Additional Lyrics

2. We bring you season's greetings as we wish the best to you,
   And may our wish last the whole year through.
   Come join us if you will as we are singing once again:

3. Now you may have your holly and perhaps some mistletoe,
   Maybe in a fir tree and maybe snow.
   But wouldn't it be wonderful if we could have again:

All My Heart This Night Rejoices

Words and Music by Johann Ebeling and Catherine Winkworth

Strum Pattern: 4
Pick Pattern: 3
Verse
Moderately

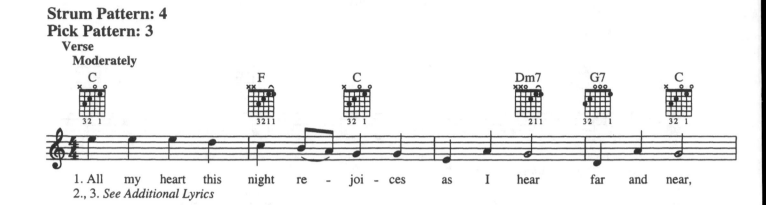

1. All my heart this night re - joi - ces as I hear far and near,
2., 3. *See Additional Lyrics*

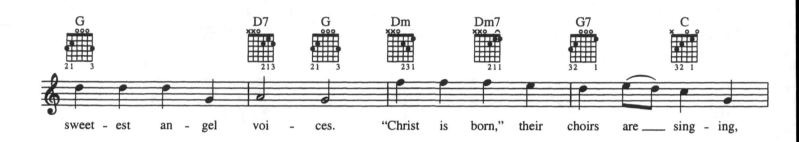

sweet - est an - gel voi - ces. "Christ is born," their choirs are ___ sing - ing,

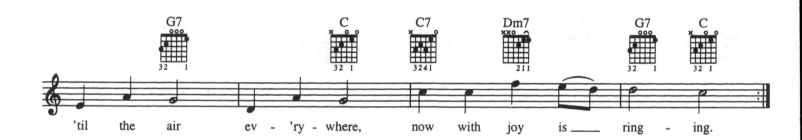

'til the air ev - 'ry - where, now with joy is ___ ring - ing.

Additional Lyrics

2. Hark! a voice from yonder manger,
   Soft and sweet doth entreat.
   "Flee from woe and danger.
   Brethren come from all that grieves you,
   You are freed.
   All you need I will surely give you."

3. Come, then, let us hasten yonder.
   Here let all, great and small,
   Kneel in awe and wonder.
   Love him who hath love is yearning.
   Hail the star that from far
   Bright with hope is burning!

All Through the Night

Welsh Folksong

Strum Pattern: 4
Pick Pattern: 3

Verse
Moderately Slow

1. Sleep, my child, and peace at - tend thee, All through the night.
2., 3. *See Additional Lyrics*

Guard - ian an - gels God will send thee, All through the night.

Soft, the drow - sy hours are creep - ing, Hill and vale in slum - ber sleep - ing.

God, his lov - ing vig - il keep - ing, All through the night.

Additional Lyrics

2. While the moon, her watch is keeping,
   All through the night.
   While the weary world is sleeping,
   All through the night.
   Through your dreams you're swiftly stealing,
   Visions of delight revealing,
   Christmas time is so appealing,
   All through the night.

3. You, my God, a babe of wonder,
   All through the night.
   Dreams you can't break from thunder,
   All through the night.
   Children's dreams cannot be broken.
   Life is but a lovely token.
   Christmas should be softly spoken,
   All through the night.

Almost Day

Words and Music by Huddie Ledbetter

Strum Pattern: 10
Pick Pattern: 10
Verse
Moderate Square Dance

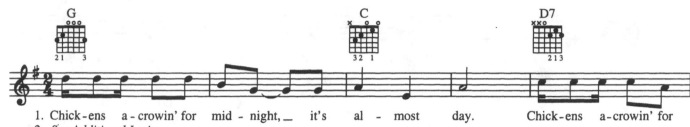

1. Chick-ens a-crowin' for mid - night, __ it's al - most day. Chick-ens a-crowin' for
2. *See Additional Lyrics*

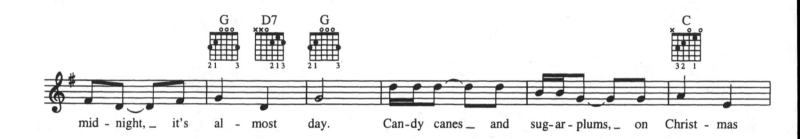

mid - night, __ it's al - most day. Can-dy canes __ and sug-ar-plums, __ on Christ - mas

Day. Can-dy canes __ and sug-ar-plums, __ on Christ - mas Day. Day.

Additional Lyrics

2. Mama'll stuff a turkey on Christmas Day.
   Mama'll stuff a turkey on Christmas Day.
   Santa Claus is coming on Christmas Day.
   Santa Claus is coming on Christmas Day.

Angels We Have Heard on High

Traditional French Carol
Translated by James Chadwick

Strum Pattern: 6
Pick Pattern: 6

Verse
Moderately

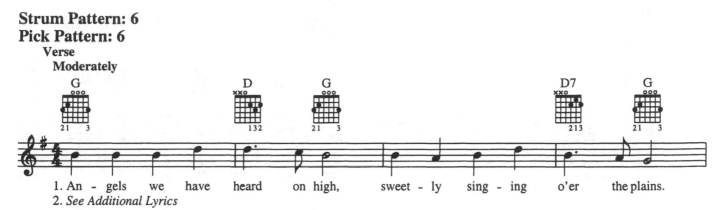

1. An - gels we have heard on high, sweet - ly sing - ing o'er the plains.
2. *See Additional Lyrics*

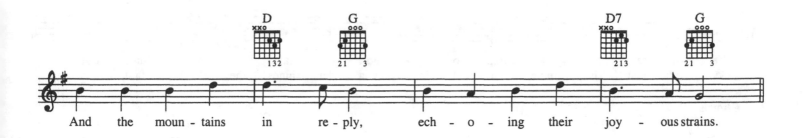

And the moun - tains in re - ply, ech - o - ing their joy - ous strains.

Chorus

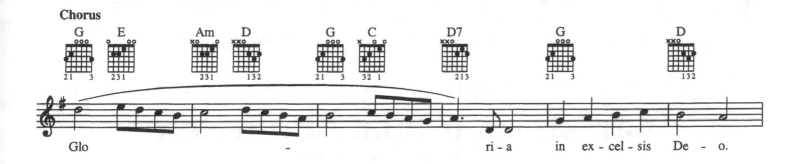

Glo - ri - a in ex - cel - sis De - o.

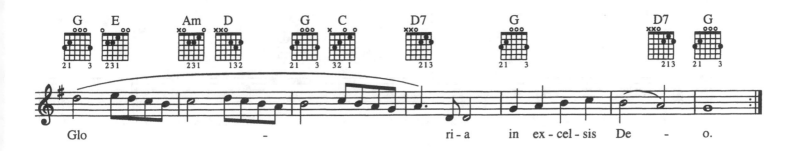

Glo - ri - a in ex - cel - sis De - o.

Additional Lyrics

2. Shepherds why this jubilee,
   Why your joyous strains prolong?
   What the gladsome tidings be
   Which inspire your heavenly song?

Angels From the Realms of Glory

Words by James Montgomery
Music by Henry T. Smart

Strum Pattern: 3
Pick Pattern: 5

Verse
Joyfully

1. An - gels from the realms of glo - ry, wing your flight o'er all the earth.
2. Shep - herds in the field a - bid - ing, watch - ing o'er your flocks by night,

Ye who sang cre - a - tion's sto - ry, now pro - claim Mes - si - ah's birth.
God with man is now re - sid - ing, yon - der shines the ___ in - fant light.

Chorus

Come and wor - ship! Come and wor - ship! Wor - ship Christ the new - born King!

Christmas Is Just About Here

Words and Music by Loonis McGlohon

Strum Pattern: 4
Pick Pattern: 3

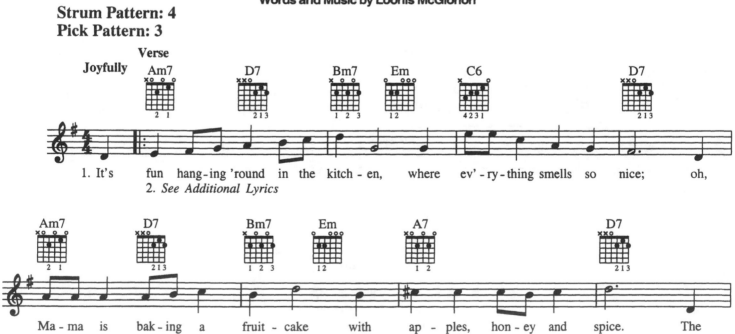

Verse
Joyfully

1. It's fun hang - ing 'round in the kitch - en, where ev' - ry - thing smells so nice; oh,
2. *See Additional Lyrics*

Ma - ma is bak - ing a fruit - cake with ap - ples, hon - ey and spice. The

Additional Lyrics

2. It's great fun when Papa will take us
To pick out a Christmas tree;
Mom says to be sure that we
Choose one that's big and taller than me.
It's time to start wrapping the presents
For ev'ryone we hold dear;
Then hiding them back in the closet
'Cause Christmas is just about here.

Chorus Deck the halls with boughs of holly,
Fill up the candy jar;
Light a candle in the window
And hang up the Christmas star.
I like ev'rything about Christmas,
The holly and the holiday cheer;
Let's hurry up and get ready
'Cause Christmas is just about here.

As Each Happy Christmas

Traditional

Strum Pattern: 4
Pick Pattern: 3

Moderately slow

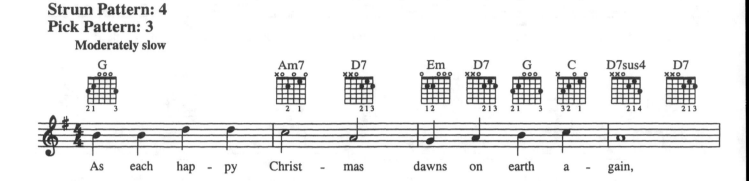

As each hap - py Christ - mas dawns on earth a - gain,

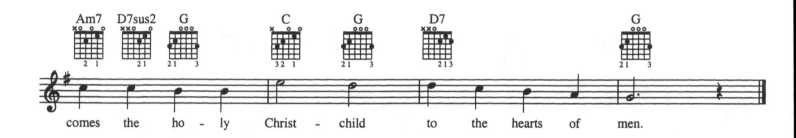

comes the ho - ly Christ - child to the hearts of men.

Christ Was Born on Christmas Day

Traditional

Strum Pattern: 8
Pick Pattern: 8

Lilting

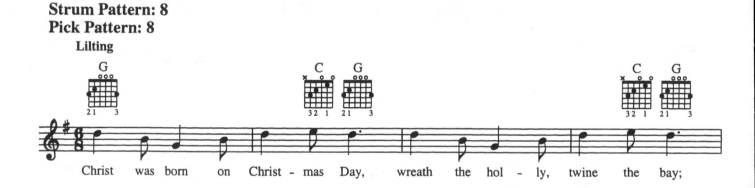

Christ was born on Christ - mas Day, wreath the hol - ly, twine the bay;

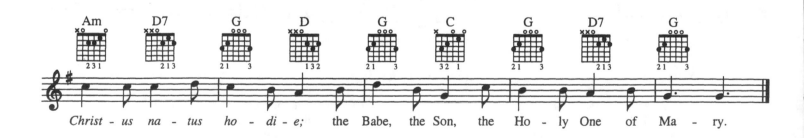

Christ - us na - tus ho - di - e; the Babe, the Son, the Ho - ly One of Ma - ry.

As Lately We Watched

19th Century Austrian Carol

Strum Pattern: 7
Pick Pattern: 7

Brightly

As late - ly we watched o'er __ our __ fields through the night, a

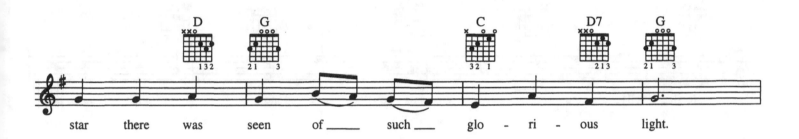

star there was seen of _____ such _____ glo - ri - ous light.

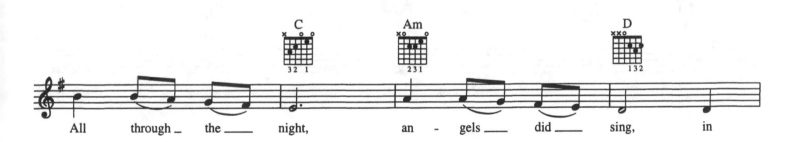

All through _ the _____ night, an - gels _____ did _____ sing, in

car - ols so sweet of _____ the _____ birth of the King.

As Long As There's Christmas

from Walt Disney's BEAUTY AND THE BEAST - THE ENCHANTED CHRISTMAS

Music by Rachel Portman
Lyrics by Don Black

Strum Pattern: 7, 8
Pick Pattern: 7, 8

Intro

Moderately Slow

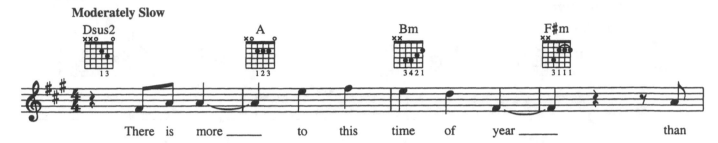

There is more _____ to this time of year _____ than

Freely

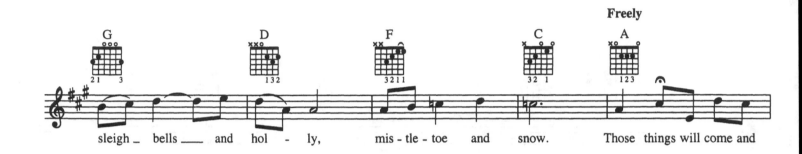

sleigh _ bells _ and hol - ly, mis - tle - toe and snow. Those things will come and

Verse
A Tempo

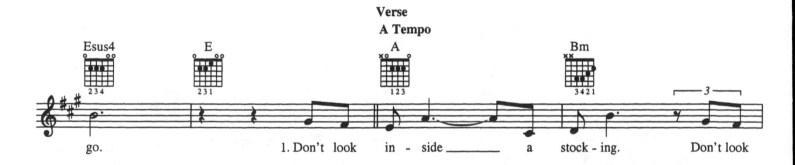

go. 1. Don't look in - side _____ a stock - ing. Don't look

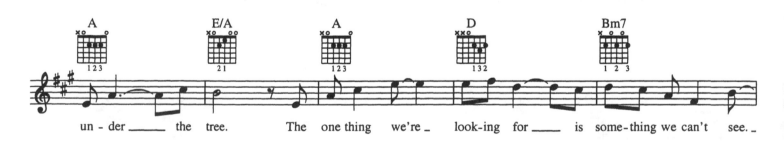

un - der _____ the tree. The one thing we're _ look-ing for _____ is some-thing we can't see. _

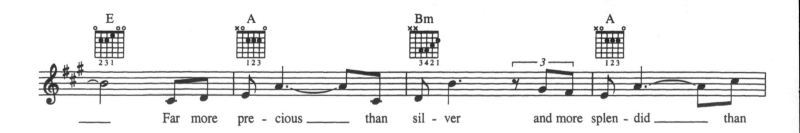

_____ Far more pre - cious _____ than sil - ver and more splen - did _____ than

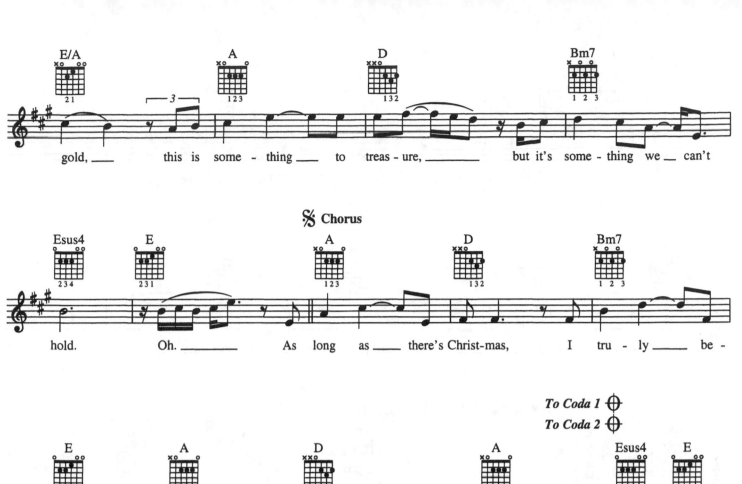

gold, _____ this is some - thing _____ to treas - ure, _____ but it's some - thing we _____ can't

𝄋 **Chorus**

hold. Oh. _____ As long as _____ there's Christ - mas, I tru - ly _____ be -

To Coda 1 ⊕
To Coda 2 ⊕

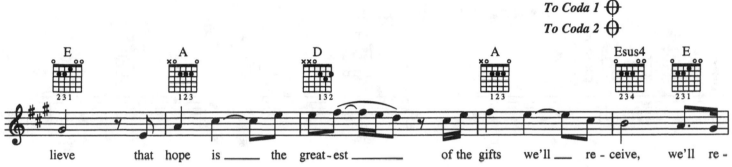

lieve that hope is _____ the great - est _____ of the gifts we'll _____ re - ceive, we'll re -

Verse

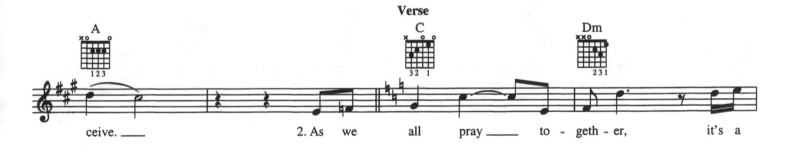

ceive. _____ 2. As we all pray _____ to - geth - er, it's a

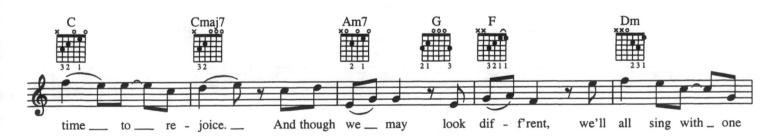

time _____ to _____ re - joice. And though we _____ may look dif - f'rent, we'll all sing with _____ one

D.S. al Coda 1

voice. Whoa. _____ As

As With Gladness Men of Old

Words by William Chatterton Dix
Music by Conrad Kocher

Strum Pattern: 4
Pick Pattern: 5

Verse
Brightly

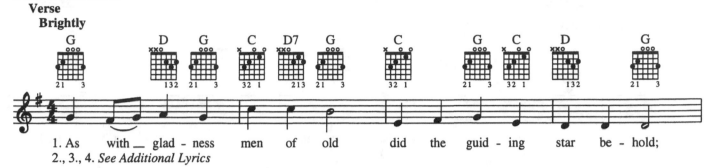

1. As with __ glad - ness men of old did the guid - ing star be - hold;
2., 3., 4. *See Additional Lyrics*

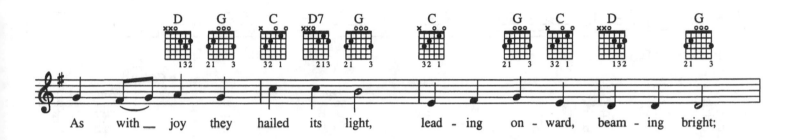

As with __ joy they hailed its light, lead - ing on - ward, beam - ing bright;

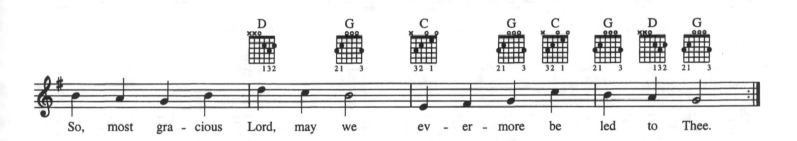

So, most gra - cious Lord, may we ev - er - more be led to Thee.

Additional Lyrics

2. As with joyful steps they sped,
   To that lowly manger bed,
   There to bend the knee before
   Him who Heaven and Earth adore,
   So may we with willing feet
   Ever seek thy mercy seat.

3. As they offered gifts most rare
   At that manger rude and bare,
   So may we with holy joy,
   Pure and free from sin's alloy,
   All our costliest treasures bring,
   Christ, to Thee, our heavenly King.

4. Holy Jesus, every day
   Keep us in the narrow way;
   And, when earthly things are past,
   Bring our ransomed souls at last
   Where they need no star to guide,
   Where no clouds Thy glory hide.

At the Hour of Midnight

Traditional

Strum Pattern: 4
Pick Pattern: 5

Additional Lyrics

2. Heaven's King eternal on the straw is lying.
   Mule and ox stand near Him; from the cold He's crying.
   Spreading hay to warm Him, ox o'er Jesus hovers;
   But the mule is wicked—he the Babe uncovers.

3. Mary weeps in pity for her suff'ring darling,
   Wishing for protection from the cold winds howling.
   "Tend'rest little Savior, O my Jesus,
   All my love forever, sweetest Son so precious."

Auld Lang Syne

Words by Robert Burns
Traditional Scottish Melody

Strum Pattern: 3
Pick Pattern: 3

Verse
Moderately

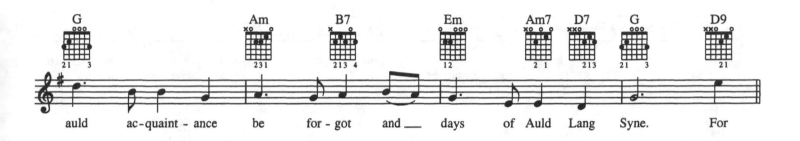

Should auld ac-quaint-ance be for-got, and ___ nev - er brought to mind? Should

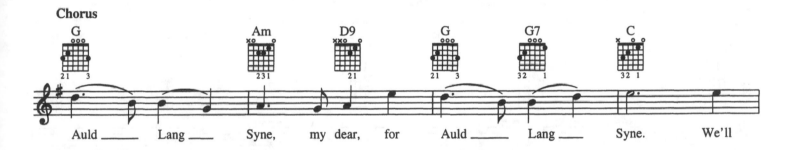

auld ac-quaint - ance be for - got and ___ days of Auld Lang Syne. For

Chorus

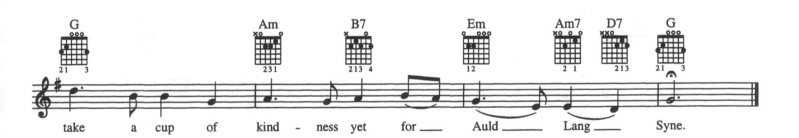

Auld ___ Lang ___ Syne, my dear, for Auld ___ Lang ___ Syne. We'll

take a cup of kind - ness yet for ___ Auld ___ Lang ___ Syne.

Ave Maria

By Franz Schubert

Strum Pattern: 1
Pick Pattern: 2

Verse
Reverently

Away in a Manger

Traditional

Music by James R. Murray

Strum Pattern: 9
Pick Pattern: 7
Verse
Sweetly

1. A - way in a man - ger, no crib for a bed, the
cat - tle are low - ing, the ba - by a - wakes, but

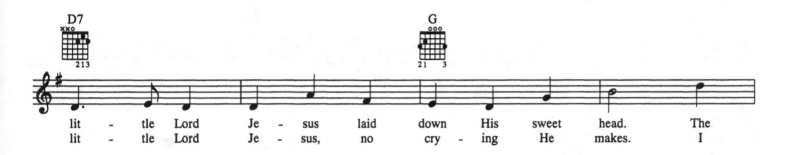

lit - tle Lord Je - sus laid down His sweet head. The
lit - tle Lord Je - sus, no cry - ing He makes. I

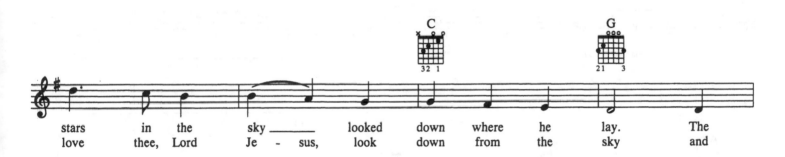

stars in the sky _____ looked down where he lay. The
love thee, Lord Je - sus, look down from the sky and

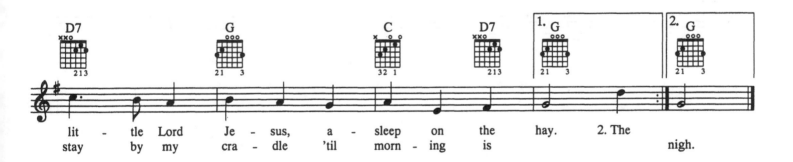

lit - tle Lord Je - sus, a - sleep on the hay. 2. The
stay by my cra - dle 'til morn - ing is nigh.

A Baby in the Cradle

By D.G. Corner

Strum Pattern: 8
Pick Pattern: 8

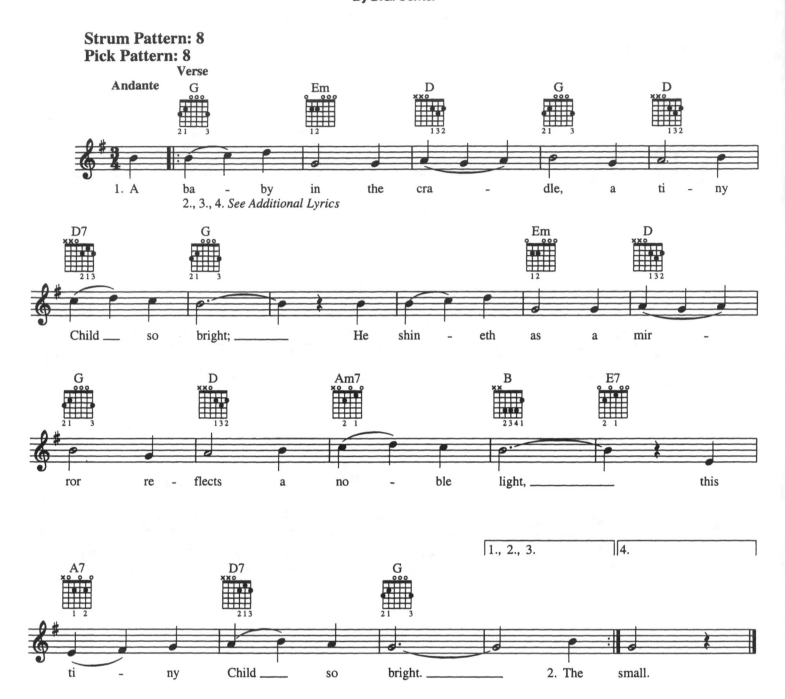

Additional Lyrics

2. The Child of whom we're speaking
   Is Jesus Christ, the Lord;
   He brings us peace and brotherhood
   If we but heed His word,
   Doth Jesus Christ, the Lord.

3. And he who rocks the cradle
   Of the sweet Child so fine
   Must serve with joy and heartiness,
   Be humble and be kind,
   For Mary's Child so fine.

4. O Jesus, dearest Savior,
   Although Thou art so small,
   With Thy great love o'erflowing
   Come flooding through my soul,
   Thou lovely Babe so small.

The Birthday of a King

Words and Music by William Neidlinger

Strum Pattern: 4
Pick Pattern: 3

Verse
Slowly

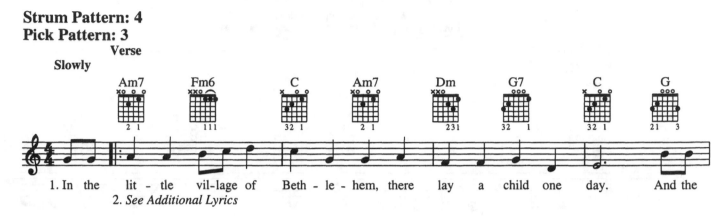

1. In the lit - tle vil-lage of Beth - le - hem, there lay a child one day. And the
2. *See Additional Lyrics*

sky was bright with a ho - ly light o'er the place where Je - sus lay. Al - le -

Chorus

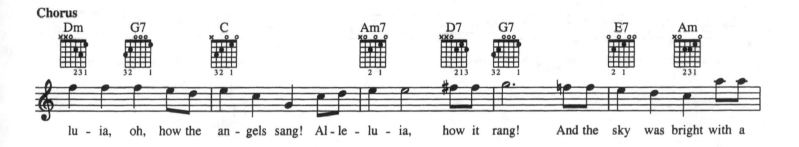

lu - ia, oh, how the an - gels sang! Al - le - lu - ia, how it rang! And the sky was bright with a

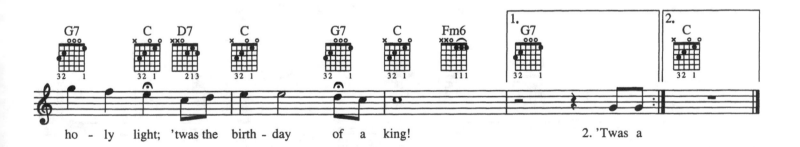

ho - ly light; 'twas the birth - day of a king!

2. 'Twas a

Additional Lyrics

2. 'Twas a humble birthplace
   But oh, how much God gave us that day!
   From the manger bed, what a path has led,
   What a perfect holy way.

Because It's Christmas
(For All the Children)

Music by Barry Manilow
Lyric by Bruce Sussman and Jack Feldman

Strum Pattern: 4
Pick Pattern: 3

Verse
Moderately Slow

Additional Lyrics

2. Tonight belongs to all the children.
   Tonight their joy rings through the air.
   And so, we send our tender blessings
   To all the children ev'rywhere
   To see the smiles and hear the laughter,
   A time to give, a time to share
   Because it's Christmas for now and forever
   For all of the children in us all.

Blue Snowfall

Words and Music by David Coleman

Strum Pattern: 4
Pick Pattern: 3

1. It's a blue snow-fall, __ for you're not here with me; it's a
2. *See Additional Lyrics*

blue snow-fall, __ through tear-filled eyes I see. 2. In a

Bridge

so. The snow bends the wil-low tree where we made a

vow, my arms held you close to me, where are you

Verse

now? 3. In these blue mo-ments __ I'm won-der-ing if

poco rit.

you see the blue snow-fall __ and if you miss me too.

2. In a blue evening,
   How slow the moments go,
   It's a blue evening,
   Because I miss you so.

Boy at a Window

Words by Arnold Sundgaard
Music by Alec Wilder

Strum Pattern: 8
Pick Pattern: 8

Bring a Torch, Jeanette, Isabella

17th Century French Provencal Carol

Strum Pattern: 8, 9
Pick Pattern: 8, 7

Verse
Brightly

Additional Lyrics

2. Hasten now, good folk of the village,
Hasten now, the Christ Child to see.
You will find him asleep in a manger,
Quitely come and whisper softly.
Hush, hush, peacefully now he slumbers,
Hush, hush, peacefully now He sleeps.

Burgundian Carol

Words and Music by Oscar Brand

Strum Pattern: 8
Pick Pattern: 8

Verse
In One

1. The win - ter sea - son of the year, when to this world our Lord was born, the
2. *See Additional Lyrics*

ox and don - key, so they say, did keep His Ho - ly Pres - ence warm.

Chorus

How man - y ox - en and don - keys now, if they were there when
See Additional Lyrics

first ___ He came? How man - y ox - en and don - keys you

know at such a time would do the same? _____

Additional Lyrics

2. As soon as to these humble beasts
   Appeared our Lord, so mild and sweet,
   With joy they knelt before His grace
   And gently kissed His tiny feet.

Chorus If we, like oxen and donkeys then,
   In spite of all the things we've heard,
   Would like to be oxen and donkeys then,
   We'd hear the truth, believe His word.

Carol of the Birds

Traditional Catalonian Carol

Strum Pattern: 10
Pick Pattern: 10

1. Up - on this ho - ly night, _____ when God's great star ap - pears, _____ and
2., 3., 4. *See Additional Lyrics*

floods the earth with bright - ness, birds' voi - ces rise in song, _____ and

warb - ling all night long, _____ ex - press their glad hearts' light - ness.

Birds' voi - ces rise _ in _ song, _____ and, warb - ling all night long, _____ ex -

press their glad heart's light - ness. _____ 2. The _____

Additional Lyrics

2. The Nightengale is first
To bring his song of cheer,
And tell us of his gladness:
"Jesus, our Lord, is born
To free us from all sin.
And banish ev'ry sadness!
Jesus, our Lord, is born
To free us from all sin,
And banish ev'ry sadness!"

3. The answ'ring Sparrow cries:
"God comes to earth this day
Amid the angels flying."
Trilling in sweetest tones,
The Finch his Lord now owns:
"To Him be all thanksgiving."
Trilling in sweetest tones,
The Finch his Lord now owns:
"To Him be all thanksgiving."

4. The Partridge adds his note:
"To Bethlehem I'll fly,
Where in the stall He's lying.
There, near the manger blest,
I'll build myself a nest.
And sing my love undying.
There, near the manger blest,
I'll build myself a nest,
And sing my love undying."

Caroling, Caroling

Words by Wihla Hutson
Music by Alfred Burt

Strum Pattern: 8
Pick Pattern: 8

Verse
With A Lilt

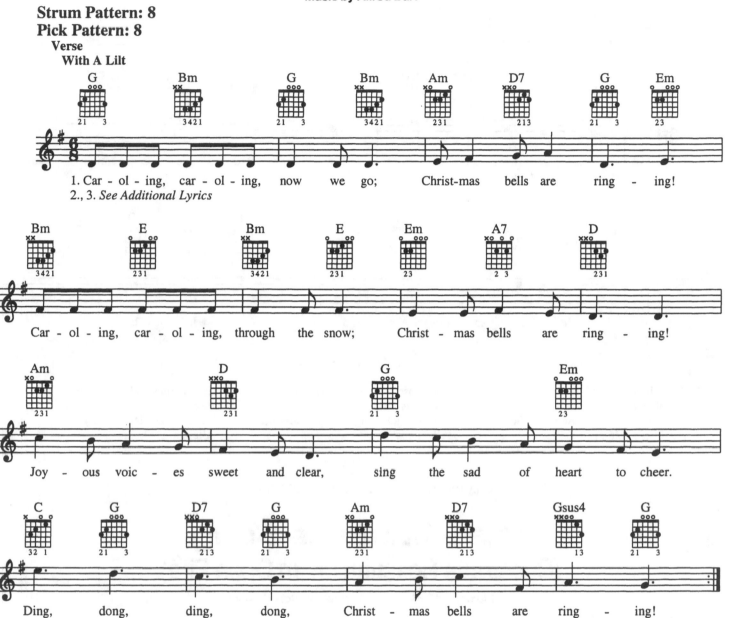

1. Car - ol - ing, car - ol - ing, now we go; Christ-mas bells are ring - ing!
2., 3. *See Additional Lyrics*

Car - ol - ing, car - ol - ing, through the snow; Christ - mas bells are ring - ing!

Joy - ous voic - es sweet and clear, sing the sad of heart to cheer.

Ding, dong, ding, dong, Christ - mas bells are ring - ing!

Additional Lyrics

2. Caroling, caroling, through the town;
   Christmas bells are ringing!
   Caroling, caroling, up and down;
   Christmas bells are ringing!
   Mark ye well the song we sing,
   Gladsome tidings now we bring.
   Ding, dong, ding, dong,
   Christmas Bells are ringing!

3. Caroling, caroling, near and far;
   Christmas bells are ringing!
   Following, following yonder star;
   Christmas bells are ringing!
   Sing we all this happy morn,
   "Lo, the King of heav'n is born!"
   Ding, dong, ding, dong,
   Christmas bells are ringing!

A Child Is Born in Bethlehem

14th-Century Latin Text adapted by Nicolai F.S. Grundtvig
Traditional Danish Melody

Strum Pattern: 4
Pick Pattern: 3

Verse
Moderately

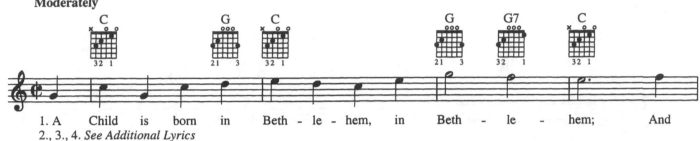

1. A Child is born in Beth - le - hem, in Beth - le - hem; And
2., 3., 4. *See Additional Lyrics*

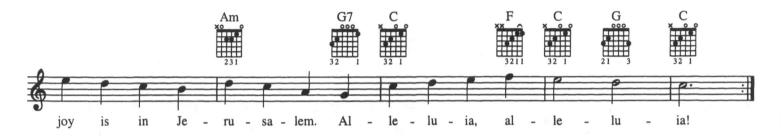

joy is in Je - ru - sa - lem. Al - le - lu - ia, al - le - lu - ia!

Additional Lyrics

2. A lowly maiden all alone,
   So all alone,
   Gave birth to God's own Holy Son.
   Alleluia, alleluia!

3. She chose a manger for His bed,
   For Jesus' bed.
   God's angels sang for joy o'erhead,
   Alleluia, alleluia!

4. Give thanks and praise eternally,
   Eternally,
   To God, the Holy Trinity.
   Alleluia, alleluia!

The Christmas Song
(Chestnuts Roasting on an Open Fire)

Music and Lyric by Mel Torme and Robert Wells

Strum Pattern: 2
Pick Pattern: 3

Verse
Sentimentally

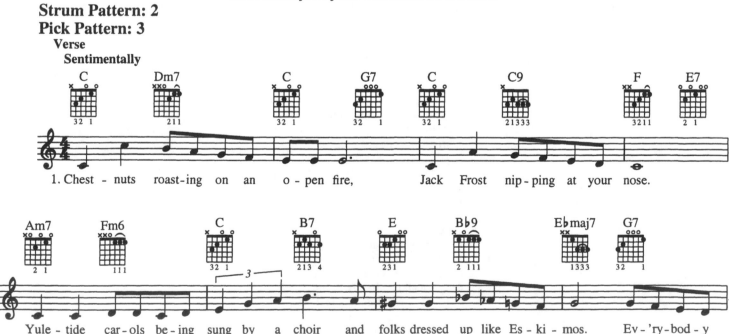

1. Chest - nuts roast - ing on an o - pen fire, Jack Frost nip - ping at your nose.

Yule - tide car - ols be - ing sung by a choir and folks dressed up like Es - ki - mos. Ev - 'ry - bod - y

knows a tur - key and some mis - tle - toe help to make the sea - son bright.

Ti - ny tots with their eyes all a - glow will find it hard to sleep to - night. They know that

Bridge

San - ta's on his way. He's load - ed lots of toys and good - ies on his sleigh. And ev - 'ry

moth - er's child __ is gon - na spy _____ to see if rein - deer _ real - ly know how to fly. 2. And

Verse

so I'm of - fer - ing this sim - ple phrase to kids from one to nine - ty - two. Al -

though it's been said man - y times, man - y ways, "Mer - ry Christ - mas to you."

The Chipmunk Song

Words and Music by Ross Bagdasarian

Strum Pattern: 8
Pick Pattern: 8

Verse
Happily

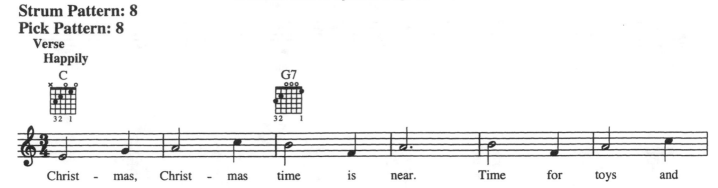

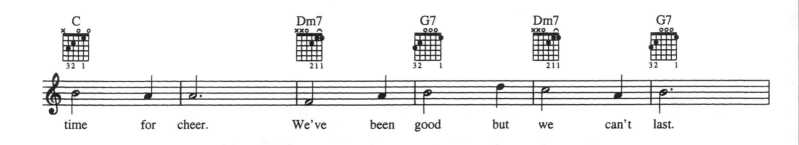

Christ - mas, Christ - mas time is near. Time for toys and

time for cheer. We've been good but we can't last.

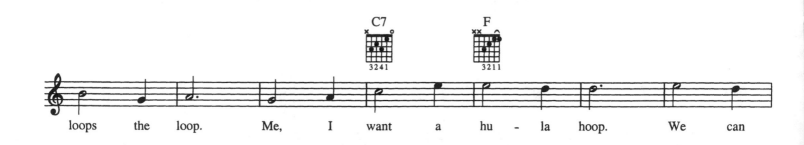

Hur - ry Christ - mas, hur - ry fast! Want a plane that

loops the loop. Me, I want a hu - la hoop. We can

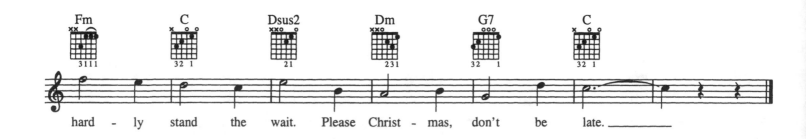

hard - ly stand the wait. Please Christ - mas, don't be late. _____

C-H-R-I-S-T-M-A-S

Words by Jenny Lou Carson
Music by Eddy Arnold

Strum Pattern: 3
Pick Pattern: 3

When I was but a young-ster, Christ-mas meant one thing; that I'd be get-ting lots of toys that day. _____ I learned a whole lot diff-'rent when Moth-er sat me down and taught me to spell Christ-mas this way. _____ "C" is for the Christ child born up-on this day, "H" for her-ald an-gels in the night. _____ "R" means our Re-deem-er, "I" means Is-ra-el. "S" is for the star that shone so bright. _____ "T" is for three wise men, they who trav-eled far. "M" is for the man-ger where He lay. _____ "A"'s for all He stands for, "S" means shep-herds came and that's why there's a Christ-mas day. _____

The Christmas Waltz

Words by Sammy Cahn
Music by Jule Styne

Strum Pattern: 9
Pick Pattern: 7

Verse
Moderately, With Expression

Come, Thou Long Expected Jesus

Words by Charles Wesley
Music adapted by Henry J. Gauntlett

Strum Pattern: 8, 7
Pick Pattern: 8, 7

Verse
Moderately

Additional Lyrics

2. Born thy people to deliver,
Born a child and yet a king.
Born to reign in us forever,
Now thy gracious kingdom bring.
By thine own eternal Spirit,
Rule in all our hearts alone.
By thine all-sufficient merit,
Raise us to thy glorious throne.

Coventry Carol

Words by Robert Croo
Traditional English Melody

Strum Pattern: 7, 9
Pick Pattern: 7, 9

Verse
Tenderly

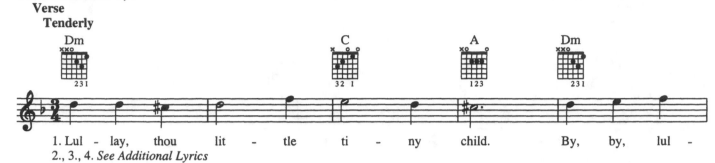

1. Lul - lay, thou lit - tle ti - ny child.   By, by, lul -
2., 3., 4. *See Additional Lyrics*

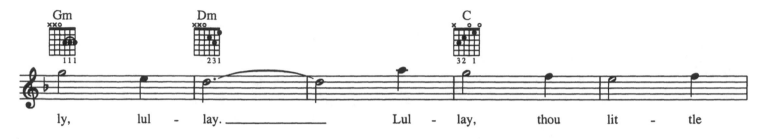

ly,   lul - lay. _____   Lul - lay,   thou   lit - tle

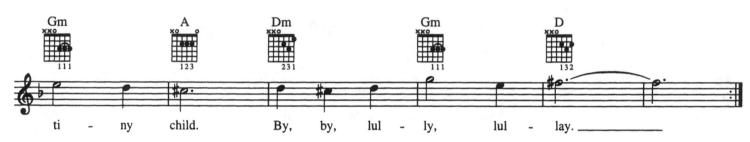

ti - ny child.   By, by, lul - ly,   lul - lay. _____

Additional Lyrics

2 Oh, sisters too,
   How may we do,
   For to preserve this day?
   This poor youngling,
   For whom we sing
   By, by, lully lullay.

3. Herod the king,
   In his raging,
   Charged he hath this day.
   His men of might,
   In his own sight,
   All young children to slay.

4. That woe is me,
   Poor child for thee!
   And ever morn and day,
   For thy parting
   Neither say nor sing
   By, by, lully lullay!

Dance of the Sugar Plum Fairy

from THE NUTCRACKER

By Pyotr Il'yich Tchaikovsky

Deck the Hall

Traditional Welsh Carol

Strum Pattern: 4, 6
Pick Pattern: 5, 6

Verse
Gaily

1. Deck the hall with boughs of hol - ly; fa, la, la, la, la, la, la, la, la.
2., 3. *See Additional Lyrics*

'Tis the sea - son to be jol - ly; fa, la, la, la, la, la, la, la, la.

Don we now our gay ap - par - el; fa, la, la, la, la, la, la, la, la.

Troll the an - cient yule - tide car - ol; fa, la, la, la, la, la, la, la, la.

Additional Lyrics

2. See the blazing yule before us;
   Fa, la, la, la, la, la, la, la, la.
   Strike the harp and join the chorus;
   Fa, la, la, la, la, la, la, la, la.
   Follow me in merry measure;
   Fa, la, la, la, la, la, la, la, la, la.
   While I tell of Yuletide treasure;
   Fa, la, la, la, la, la, la, la, la.

3. Fast away the old year passes;
   Fa, la, la, la, la, la, la, la, la.
   Hail the new ye lads and lasses;
   Fa, la, la, la, la, la, la, la, la.
   Sing we joyous, all together;
   Fa, la, la, la, la, la, la, la, la.
   Heedless of the wind and weather;
   Fa, la, la, la, la, la, la, la, la.

Ding Dong! Merrily on High!

French Carol

Strum Pattern: 2
Pick Pattern: 4

Verse
Moderately

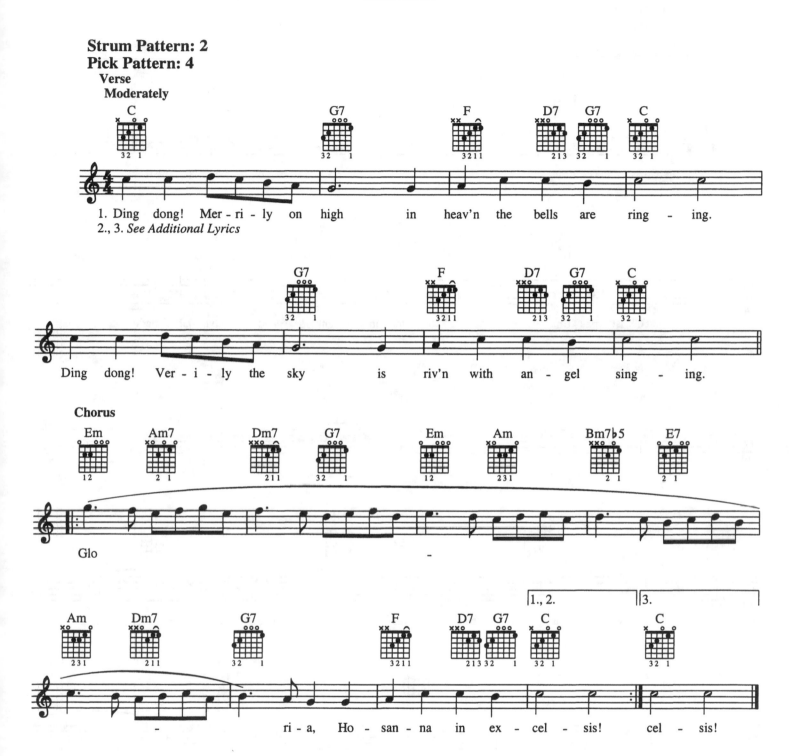

1. Ding dong! Mer - ri - ly on high   in heav'n the bells are ring - ing.
2., 3. *See Additional Lyrics*

Ding dong! Ver - i - ly the sky   is riv'n with an - gel sing - ing.

Chorus

Glo - - ri - a, Ho - san - na in ex - cel - sis!   cel - sis!

Additional Lyrics

2. E'en so here below, below
   Let steeple bells be swingen,
   And i - o, i - o, i - o
   By priest and people sungen.

3. Pray you dutifully prime
   Your main chime, ye ringers;
   May you beautiful rime
   Your evetime song, ye singers.

Do They Know It's Christmas?

Words and Music by M. Ure and B. Geldof

Strum Pattern: 3, 4
Pick Pattern: 3, 4
Verse
Medium Rock In Two

there's __ a __ world out - side your win - dow, __ and it's a world of __ dread and fear __

__ where the on - ly wa - ter flow-ing is __ the bit - ter sting of

tears.   And the Christ-mas bells __ that ring __ there __ are the clang-ing chimes of doom.

__   Well, to - night thank God it's them __ in - stead of you. __

And there won't be snow __ in Af - ri - ca __ this Christ - mas - time, __

the great-est gift __ they'll get this year __ is life. __   Oh. __

__ Where noth-ing ev - er grows, __   no rain or riv - ers flow, __

43

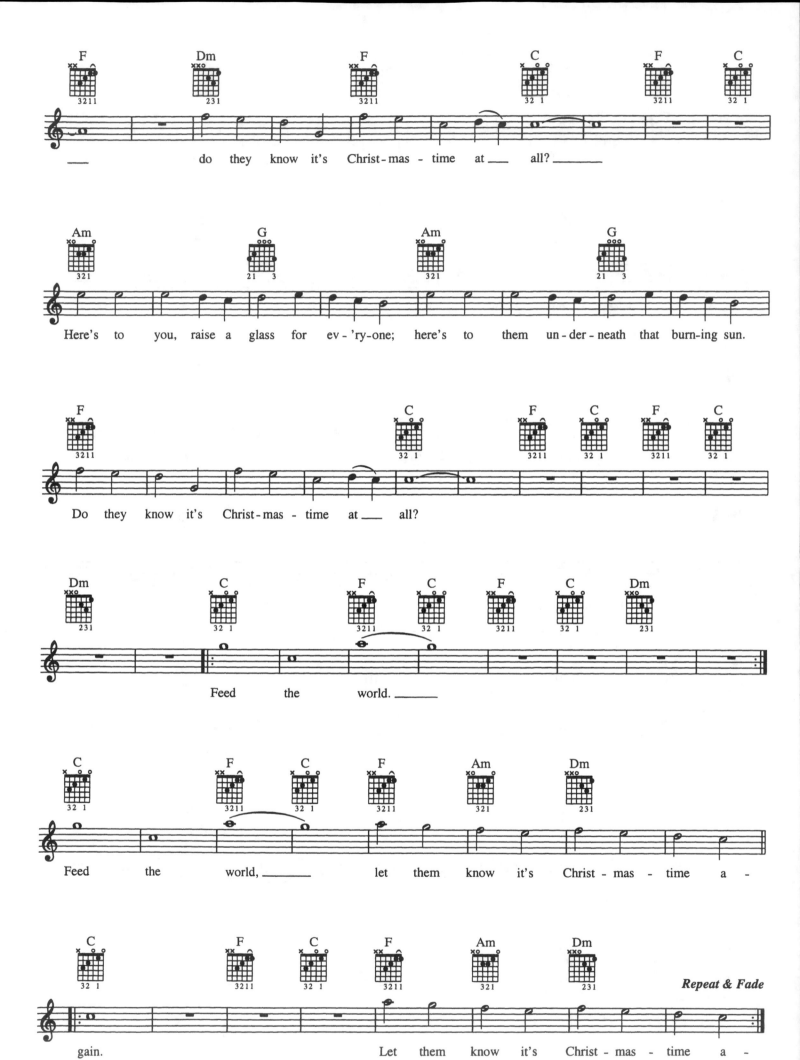

do they know it's Christ-mas - time at ___ all? _____

Here's to you, raise a glass for ev-'ry-one; here's to them un-der-neath that burn-ing sun.

Do they know it's Christ-mas - time at ___ all?

Feed the world. _____

Feed the world, _____ let them know it's Christ-mas - time a -

Repeat & Fade

gain. Let them know it's Christ-mas - time a -

Don't Make Me Play
That Grandma Song Again

Words and Music by Elmo Shropshire and Rita Abrams

Strum Pattern: 4
Pick Pattern: 3

an - y thing you say, I'll play those bark - in' dogs __ all day, but please don't make me play that

grand - ma song a - gain! __

Verse

3. Friends! It's that time of year a - gain that makes you just wan - na get out there and

charge! And while you're do - in' it, why not have, play - in' in the back - ground, our col -

lec - tor's set of twen - ty four of the most be - lov - ed Christ - mas Car - ols of all

time. Clas - sics like "You Bumped Your Nog - in' on My To - bog - gin" or,

"Hey! Hey! Gram - pa's Got a Brand New Nag!" __ To or - der now dial

*Sing like grandmas.

Additional Lyrics

2. *Spoken: Now, ev'ry Christmas I get frosted,*
When poor Grandma got acosted,
And all them wierdos enjoy her suffering.
And that Elmo guy just keeps on smilin'
While them royalties keep on pilin' and the worst part is...
He can't even sing!

Everyone's a Child at Christmas

Music and Lyrics by Johnny Marks

Strum Pattern: 4
Pick Pattern: 3

Verse
Moderately

Everywhere, Everywhere, Christmas Tonight

By Lewis H. Redner and Phillip Brooks

Strum Pattern: 7
Pick Pattern: 7

1. Christ - mas in lands of the fir tree and pine, Christ - mas in
2. *See Additional Lyrics*

lands of the palm tree and vine, Christ - mas where snow peaks stand

sol - emn and white Christ - mas where corn - fields lie sun - ny and

bright. Ev - 'ry - where, ev - 'ry - where, Christ - mas to - night. night.

Additional Lyrics

2. Christmas where children are hopeful and gay,
Christmas where old men are patient and gray,
Christmas where peace like a dove in its flight
Broods o'er brave men in the thick of the fight.
Ev'rywhere, ev'rywhere, Christmas tonight.

Feels Like Christmas

Words and Music by Pam Wendell and Elmo Shropshire

Strum Pattern: 5
Pick Pattern: 1

Intro
Moderately Slow

1. Old Saint Nick and Miss - es Claus _ de - cid - ed just _ this year, _ there
2. *See Additional Lyrics*

won't be an - y Christ-mas, the feel-ing's just _ not here. _

Some kids get more than _ they need; some are spoil - ed rot - ten, and

when it comes _ to Christ-mas time too man - y are for - got-ten. It will

Chorus

feel like Christ-mas to peo-ple ev-'ry-where. __ It will

1.

feel like Christ-mas when we all learn to share. _ 2. So

2.   **Guitar Solo**

we all learn to share. _

Then

Bridge

all the kids _ said, "San-ta Claus, _ we have too man-y toys. __ We'd

like to share _ our bless-ings _ with oth-er girls _ and boys." __ 1. Now it

Outro

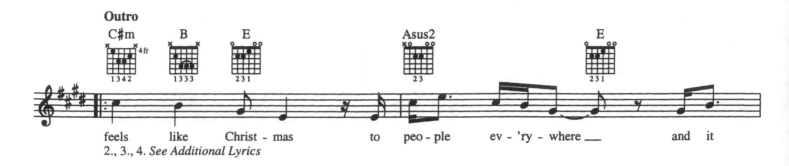

feels   like   Christ - mas   to   peo - ple   ev - 'ry - where ___   and   it

2., 3., 4. *See Additional Lyrics*

feels   like   Christ - mas   be - cause   we   learned _   to   share. _   2. It   will

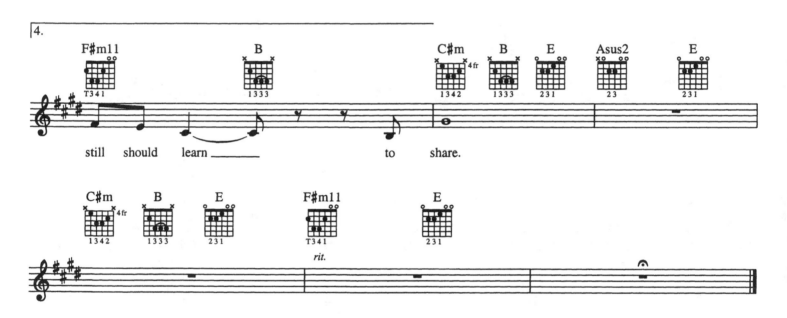

still   should   learn _____   to   share.

rit.

Additional Lyrics

2. So Santa said to Mrs. Claus,
   "Something's way off track,
   I can't get into Christmas until the spirit's back.
   If there was just a way we could
   Get boys and girls to see,
   Christmas is what's in our heart
   And not what's 'neath the tree."

Outro 2.   It will feel like Christmas
            To people ev'rywhere.
            It will feel like Christmas
            When we all learn to share.

Outro 3. *Spoken: And will it feel like Christmas*
            When we've new things to wear? No.
            It will feel like Christmas
            When we all learn to share.

Outro 4. *Spoken: And it will feel like Christmas*
            When Dr. Elmo is on the air?
            Oh, yes. It will feel like Christmas
            But we still should learn to share.

Feliz Navidad

Music and Lyrics by Jose Feliciano

Strum Pattern: 2, 1
Pick Pattern: 4, 2

The First Noel

17th Century English Carol
Music from W. Sandys' Christmas Carols

Strum Pattern: 7, 8
Pick Pattern: 9, 8

Verse
Moderately Slow

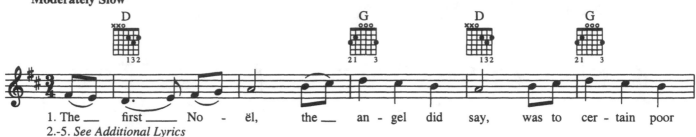

1. The __ first ____ No - ël, the __ an - gel did say, was to cer - tain poor
2.-5. *See Additional Lyrics*

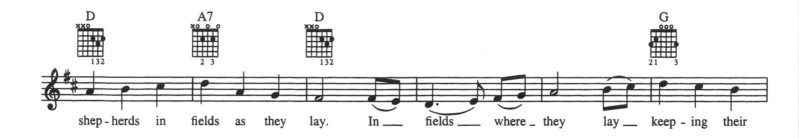

shep - herds in fields as they lay. In __ fields ____ where __ they lay __ keep - ing their

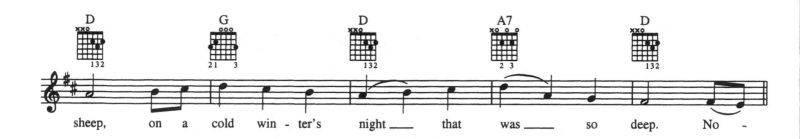

sheep, on a cold win - ter's night ____ that was ____ so deep. No -

Chorus

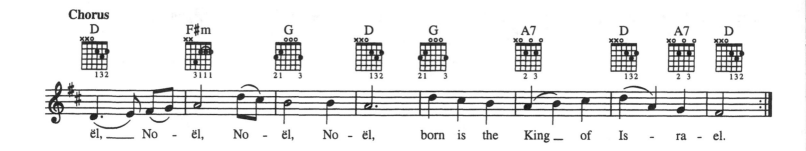

ël, ____ No - ël, No - ël, No - ël, born is the King __ of Is - ra - el.

Additional Lyrics

2. They looked up and saw a star
   Shining in the East, beyond them far.
   And to the earth it gave great light
   And so it continued both day and night.

3. And by the light of that same star,
   Three wise man came from country far;
   To seek for a King was their intent,
   And to follow the star wherever it went.

4. This star drew nigh to the northwest,
   O'er Bethlehem it took its rest;
   And there it did both stop and stay,
   Right over the place where Jesus lay.

5. Then entered in those wise men three,
   Full reverently upon their knee;
   And offered there in His presence,
   Their gold, and myrrh, and frankincense.

The Friendly Beasts

Traditional English Carol

Strum Pattern: 8
Pick Pattern: 9

Verse
Moderately

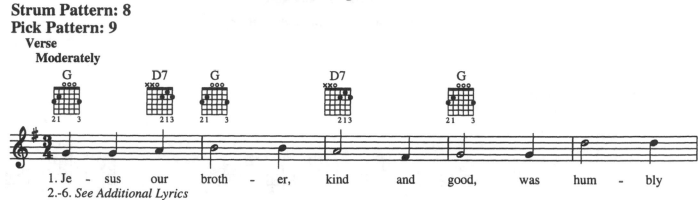

1. Je - sus our broth - er, kind and good, was hum - bly
2.-6. *See Additional Lyrics*

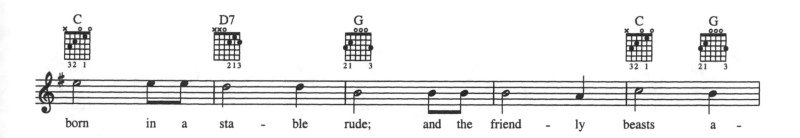

born in a sta - ble rude; and the friend - ly beasts a -

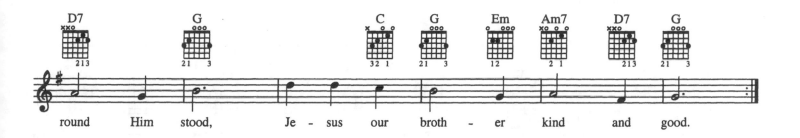

round Him stood, Je - sus our broth - er kind and good.

Additional Lyrics

2. "I," said the donkey, shaggy and brown,
   "I carried his mother up hill and down.
   I carried his mother to Bethlehem town."
   "I," said the donkey, shaggy and brown.

3. "I," said the cow, all white and red,
   "I gave Him my manger for His bed;
   I gave Him my hay to pillow His head."
   "I," said the cow, all white and red.

4. "I," said the sheep with the curly horn,
   "I gave Him my wool for His blanket warm;
   He wore my coat on Christmas morn."
   "I," said the sheep with the curly horn.

5. "I," said the dove from the rafters high,
   "I cooed Him to sleep that He would not cry;
   We cooed Him to sleep, my mate and I."
   "I," said the dove from the rafters high.

6. Thus every beast by some good spell,
   In the stable dark was glad to tell
   Of the gift he gave Emmanuel,
   The gift he gave Emmanuel.

From Heaven Above to Earth I Come

Words and Music by Martin Luther

Strum Pattern: 4
Pick Pattern: 3

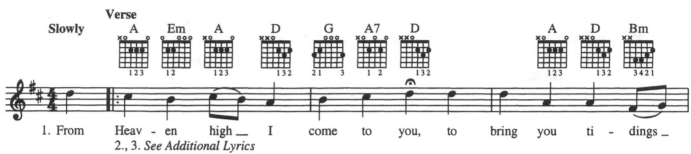

Slowly   Verse

1. From Heav - en high __ I come to you, to bring you ti - dings __
2., 3. *See Additional Lyrics*

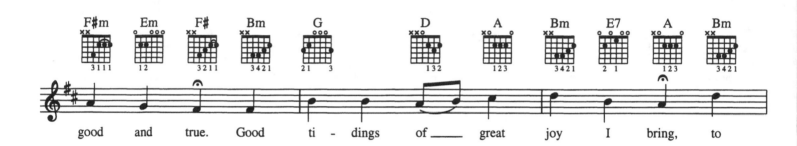

good and true. Good ti - dings of ____ great joy I bring, to

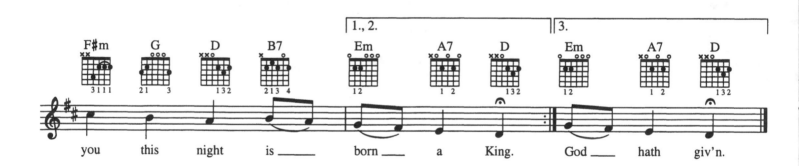

you this night is ____ born ___ a King.   God ____ hath giv'n.

Additional Lyrics

2. This King is but a little child,
   His mother blessed Mary mild.
   His cradle is but now a stall,
   Yet He brings joy and peace to all.

3. Now let us all with songs of cheer,
   Follow the shepherds and draw near,
   To find the wondrous gift of Heav'n,
   The Blessed Christ whom God hath giv'n.

Fum, Fum, Fum

Traditional Catalonian Carol

Strum Pattern: 4
Pick Pattern: 3

Verse
Brightly

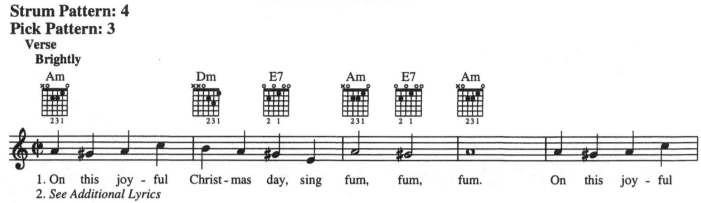

1. On this joy - ful Christ - mas day, sing fum, fum, fum. On this joy - ful
2. *See Additional Lyrics*

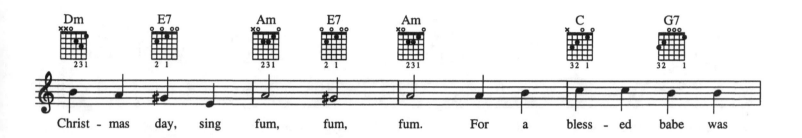

Christ - mas day, sing fum, fum, fum. For a bless - ed babe was

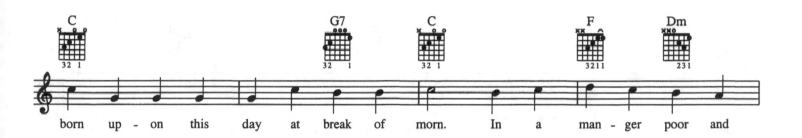

born up - on this day at break of morn. In a man - ger poor and

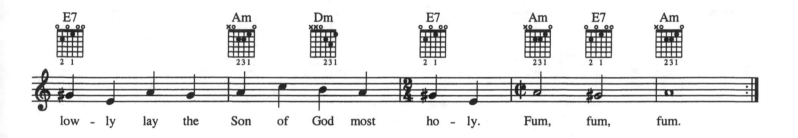

low - ly lay the Son of God most ho - ly. Fum, fum, fum.

Additional Lyrics

2. Thanks to God for holidays, sing fum, fum, fum.
   Thanks to God for holidays, sing fum, fum, fum.
   Now we all our voices raise.
   And sing a song of grateful praise.
   Celebrate in song and story, all the wonders of his glory.
   Fum, fum, fum.

Frosty the Snow Man

Words and Music by Steve Nelson and Jack Rollins

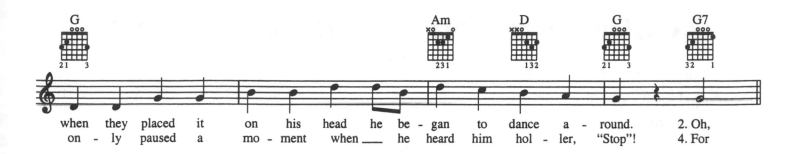

when they placed it on his head he be - gan to dance a - round. 2. Oh,
on - ly paused a mo - ment when ___ he heard him hol - ler, "Stop"! 4. For

Verse

Frost - y the snow man was a - live as he could be, and the
Frost - y the snow man had to hur - ry on his way, but he

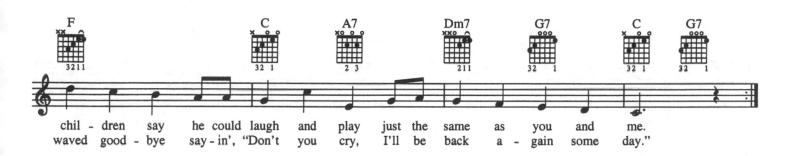

chil - dren say he could laugh and play just the same as you and me.
waved good - bye say - in', "Don't you cry, I'll be back a - gain some day."

Outro

Thup - et - y thump thump, thump-et - y thump thump, look at Frost - y go.

Thump-et - y thump thump, thump-et - y thump thump, o - ver the hills of snow.

Gather Around the Christmas Tree

By John H. Hopkins

Strum Pattern: 4
Pick Pattern: 5

Verse
Lively

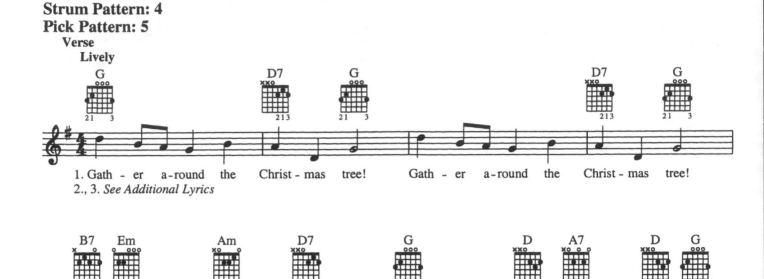

1. Gath - er a-round the Christ - mas tree! Gath - er a-round the Christ - mas tree!
2., 3. *See Additional Lyrics*

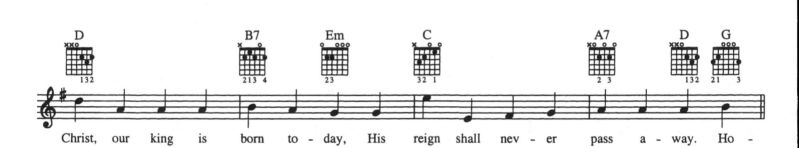

Ev - er green have its branch - es been, it is king of all the wood - land scene. For

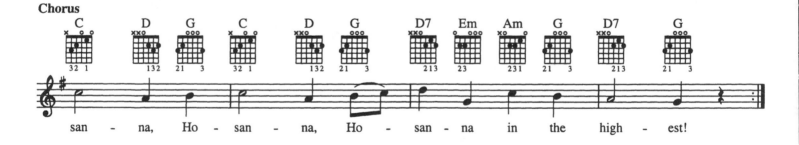

Christ, our king is born to - day, His reign shall nev - er pass a - way. Ho -

Chorus

san - na, Ho - san - na, Ho - san - na in the high - est!

Additional Lyrics

2. Gather around the Christmas tree!
   Gather around the Christmas tree!
   Once the pride of the mountainside,
   Now cut down to grace our Christmastide.
   For Christ from heav'n to earth came down
   To gain, through death, a nobler crown.

3. Gather around the Christmas tree!
   Gather around the Christmas tree!
   Ev'ry bough has a burden now,
   They are gifts of love for us, we trow.
   For Christ is born, his love to show
   And give good gifts to men below.

Go, Tell It on the Mountain

African-American Spiritual
Verses by John W. Work, Jr.

Additional Lyrics

2. The shepherds feared and trembled
   When, lo! above the earth
   Rang out the angel chorus
   That hailed our Savior's birth.

3. Down in a lowly manger
   Our humble Christ was born.
   And God sent us salvation
   That blessed Christmas morn.

The Gift

Words and Music by Tom Douglas and Jim Brickman

You saved my heart _____ from be - ing bro - ken a - part.

You gave your love a - way and I'm thank - ful ev - 'ry day __

for the gift.

Verse

2. Watch - ing as you

soft - ly __ sleep, what I'd give if I could _ keep just the mo -

- ment, if on - ly time _ stood still. But the col - ors fade _

_____ a - way and the years will make us __ gray, _ but, ba - by, in my __

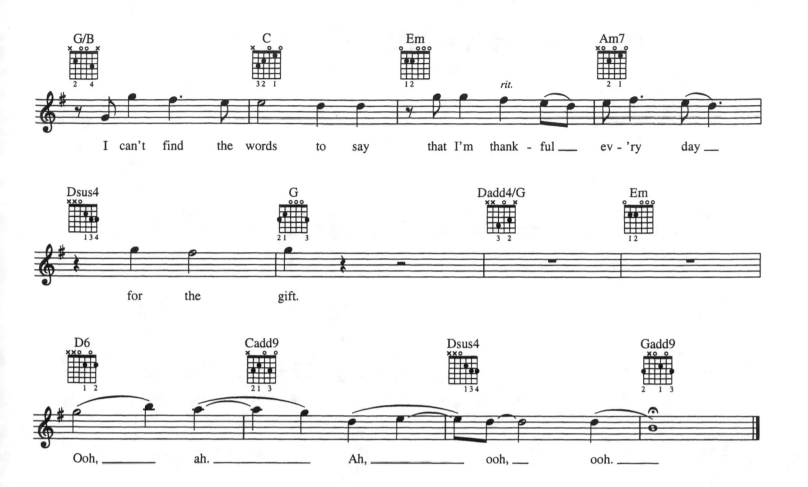

I can't find the words to say that I'm thank-ful ___ ev-'ry day ___

for the gift.

Ooh, ___ ah. ___ Ah, ___ ooh, ___ ooh. ___

Glad Tidings
(Shalom Chaverim)

English Lyrics and New Music Arranged by Ronnie Gilbert, Lee Hays, Fred Hellerman and Pete Seeger

Strum Pattern: 4
Pick Pattern: 3

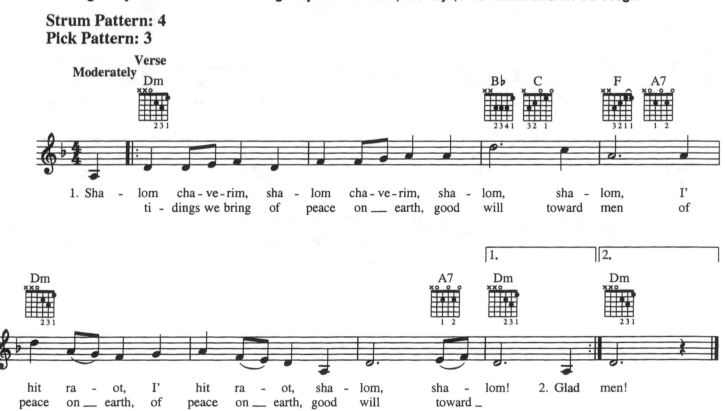

1. Sha - lom cha - ve - rim, sha - lom cha - ve - rim, sha - lom, sha - lom, I'
   ti - dings we bring of peace on ___ earth, good will toward men of

hit ra - ot, I' hit ra - ot, sha - lom, sha - lom! 2. Glad men!
peace on ___ earth, of peace on ___ earth, good will toward ___

God Rest Ye Merry, Gentlemen

19th Century English Carol

Strum Pattern: 3, 5
Pick Pattern: 3, 4

Verse
Moderately

1. God rest ye mer - ry, gen - tle - men, let noth - ing you dis - may. For
2. *See Additional Lyrics*

Je - sus Christ our Sav - ior was born up - on this day, to

save us all from Sa - tan's power when we were gone a - stray. O _____

Chorus

tid - ings of com - fort and joy, com - fort and joy. O _____

tid - ings of com - fort and joy! 2. In joy!

Additional Lyrics

2. In Bethlehem, in Jewry
This blessed babe was born
And laid within a manger
Upon this blessed morn
To which His mother Mary
Did nothing take in scorn.

Good Christian Men, Rejoice

14th Century Latin Text
Translated by John Mason Neale
14th Century German Melody

Strum Pattern: 9
Pick Pattern: 7

Verse
With Spirit

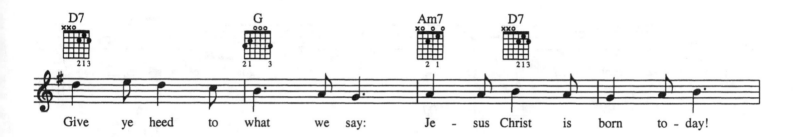

1. Good Chris - tian men, re - joice _____ with heart and soul and voice. _____
2. *See Additional Lyrics*

Give ye heed to what we say: Je - sus Christ is born to - day!

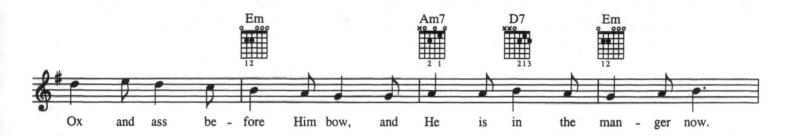

Ox and ass be - fore Him bow, and He is in the man - ger now.

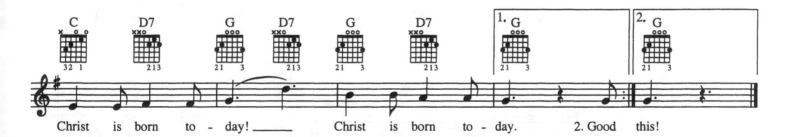

Christ is born to - day! _____ Christ is born to - day. 2. Good this!

Additional Lyrics

2. Good Christian men, rejoice
   With heart and soul and voice.
   Now ye hear of endless bliss:
   Jesus Christ was born for this!
   He hath op'd the heavenly door,
   And man is blessed evermore.
   Christ was born for this!
   Christ was born for this!

Goin' on a Sleighride

Words and Music by Ralph Blane

Strum Pattern: 10
Pick Pattern: 10
Verse
Moderately Fast

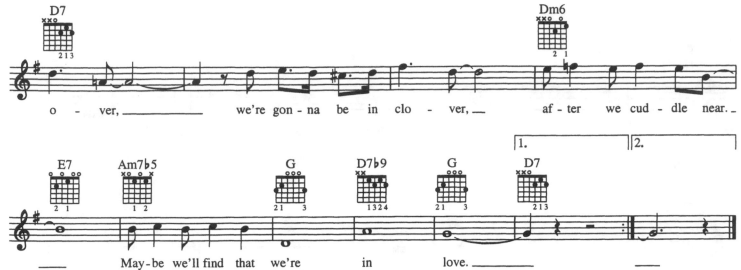

o - ver, _____ we're gon - na be in clo - ver, _____ af - ter we cud - dle near. _____

May - be we'll find that we're in love. _____

Grandma's Killer Fruitcake

Words and Music by Elmo Shropshire and Rita Abrams

Strum Pattern: 3
Pick Pattern: 5

Intro
Country Polka

1. The

Verse

hol - i - days were up - on us and things were go - in' fine, 'til the

day I heard the door - bell and a chill ran up my spine. I

grabbed the wife and chil - dren as the post - man wheeled it in. A

year - ly Christ - mas night - mare has just come back a - gain. It was

Chorus

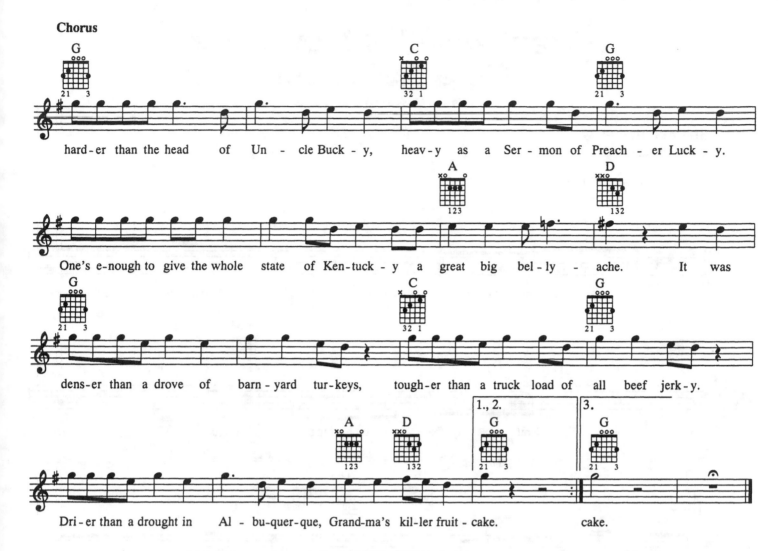

hard-er than the head of Un-cle Buck-y, heav-y as a Ser-mon of Preach-er Luck-y.

One's e-nough to give the whole state of Ken-tuck-y a great big bel-ly - ache. It was

dens-er than a drove of barn-yard tur-keys, tough-er than a truck load of all beef jerk-y.

Dri-er than a drought in Al - bu-quer-que, Grand-ma's kil-ler fruit - cake. cake.

Additional Lyrics

2. Now I've had to swallow some marginal fare at our family feast.
   I even downed Aunt Dolly's possom pie just to keep the family peace.
   I winced at Wilma's gizzard mousse, but said it tasted fine,
   But that lethal weapon that Grandma bakes is where I draw the line.

3. It's early Christmas morning, the phone rings us awake.
   It's Grandma, Pa, she wants to know how'd we like the cake.
   "Well, Grandma, I never. Uh we couldn't. It was, uh, unbelievable, that's for shore.
   What's that you say? Oh, no Grandma, Puh-leez don't send us more!"

Grandma Got Run Over By a Reindeer

Words and Music by Randy Brooks

Strum Pattern: 3
Pick Pattern: 3

Chorus
Moderately Bright

Grand-ma got run o-ver by a rein-deer walk-ing home from our house Christ-mas

Eve. You can say there's no such thing as San-ta, but

To Coda ⊕   **Verse**

as for me and Grand-pa, we be-lieve. 1. She'd been drink-ing too much
2., 3. *See Additional Lyrics*

egg-nog and we begged her not to go.

But she for-got her med-i-ca-tion, and she stag-gered out the door in-to the

snow. When we found her Christ-mas morn-ing

at the scene of the at - tack,   she had hoof-prints on her

fore-head,   and in - crim - i - nat - ing Claus marks on her back.   elves.

⊕ Coda

Outro-Chorus

lieve.   Grand - ma   got   run   o - ver   by   a   rein - deer

walk - ing home from our house Christ-mas   Eve.   You   can   say there's   no   such thing as

San - ta,   but   as   for me and Grand-pa, we be - lieve. _____

Additional Lyics

2. Now we're all so proud of Grandpa.
   He's been taking it so well.
   See him in there watching football,
   Drinking beer and playing cards with Cousin Mel.
   It's not Christmas without Grandma.
   All the family's dressed in black,
   And we just can't help but wonder:
   Should we open up her gifts or send them back?

3. Now the goose is on the table,
   And the pudding made of fig.
   And the blue and silver candles,
   That would just have matched the hair in Grandma's wig.
   I've warned all my friends and neighbors.
   Better watch out for yourselves.
   They should never give a license
   To a man who drives a sleigh and plays with elves.

Good King Wenceslas

Words by John M. Neale
Music from Piae Cantiones

Strum Pattern: 4, 3
Pick Pattern: 5, 3

Verse
With Spirit

1. Good King Wen - ces - las looked out on the feast of Ste - phen;
2.-5. *See Additional Lyrics*

when the snow lay 'round a - bout, deep and crisp and e - ven.

Bright - ly shone the moon that night, though the frost was cru - el;

when a poor man came in sight, gath - 'ring win - ter fu - el.

Additional Lyrics

2. "Hither page, and stand by me,
   If thou know'st it, telling;
   Yonder peasant, who is he?
   Where and what his dwelling?"
   "Sire, he lives a good league hence,
   Underneath the mountain;
   Right against the forest fence,
   By Saint Agnes' fountain."

3. "Bring me flesh, and bring me wine,
   Bring me pine-logs hither;
   Thou and I will see him dine,
   When we bear them thither."
   Page and monarch forth they went,
   Forth they went together;
   Through the rude winds wild lament,
   And the bitter weather.

4. "Sire, the night is darker now,
   And the wind blows stronger;
   Fails my heart, I know not how,
   I can go not longer."
   "Mark my footsteps, my good page,
   Tread thou in them boldly:
   Thou shalt find the winter's rage
   Freeze thy blood less coldly."

5. In his master's steps he trod,
   Where the snow lay dinted;
   Heat was in the very sod
   Which the saint has printed.
   Therefore, Christian men, be sure,
   Wealth or rank possessing;
   Ye who now will bless the poor,
   Shall yourselves find blessing.

Greenwillow Christmas

from GREENWILLOW

By Frank Loesser

Strum Pattern: 4
Pick Pattern: 3

Verse
Moderately

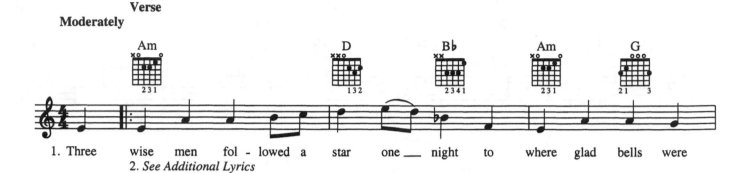

1. Three wise men fol-lowed a star one __ night to where glad bells were
2. *See Additional Lyrics*

peel - ing, _____ and soon be-held the __ Ho - ly __ Child and

Chorus

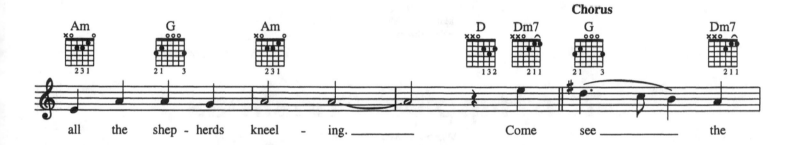

all the shep - herds kneel - ing. _____ Come see _____ the

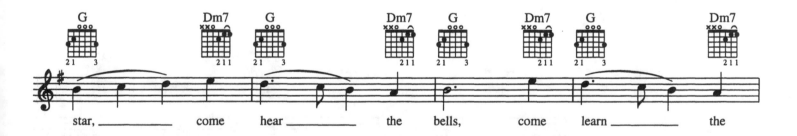

star, _____ come hear _____ the bells, come learn _____ the

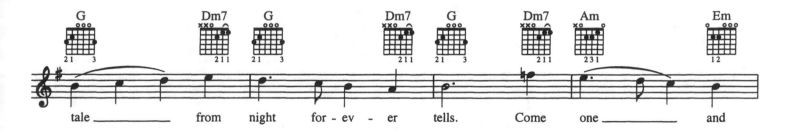

tale _____ from night for - ev - er tells. Come one _____ and

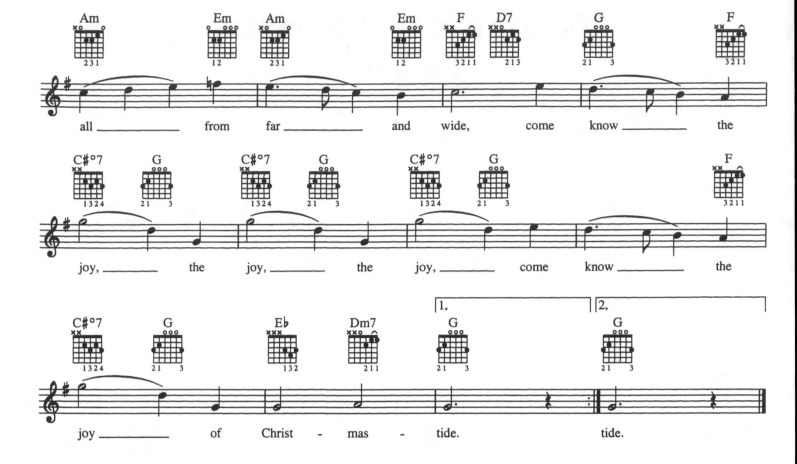

all ___ from far ___ and wide, come know ___ the

joy, ___ the joy, ___ the joy, ___ come know ___ the

1. 2.

joy ___ of Christ - mas - tide. tide.

Additional Lyrics

2. 'Twas long ago in Bethlehem
   Yet ever live the glory,
   And hearts all glow and voices rise
   A-caroling the story.

The Happiest Christmas

Words by Miles Rudge
Music by Ted Dicks

Strum Pattern: 4
Pick Pattern: 3

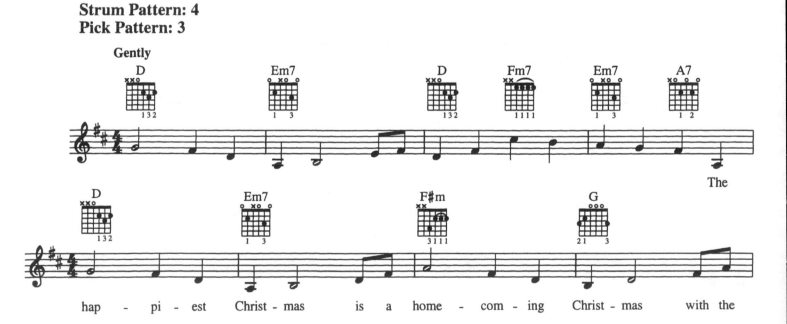

Gently

The

hap - pi - est Christ - mas is a home - com - ing Christ - mas with the

snow   flut - t'ring down   till the world   seems   new. ____

____   Bright can - dles   burn - ing, ____   old friends re -

turn - ing, ____   the wish - es ____ of chil - dren com - ing true. ____

____   And the hap - pi - est wish - es   are just old - fash - ioned

wish - es, may your days   be mer - ry, ____ your sor - rows ____ be

small. ____   May the ones   you   love   be

near you, __ that's the hap - pi - est Christ - mas __ of all. ____

The Greatest Gift of All

Words and Music by John Jarvis

Strum Pattern: 4, 3
Pick Pattern: 5, 3
Verse
Moderately Slow

Through the win - dow I ___ can see ___ snow be - gin to fall.

Know-ing you're in ___ love with me ___ is the great - est gift of ___ all.

Verse

3. Just be - fore I go to sleep ___ I hear a church bell ring.

Mer - ry Christ - mas ev - 'ry - one ___ is the song it ___ sings.

So I say a si - lent prayer ___ for crea - tures great and small.

Peace on earth good _ will to men is the great - est gift of ___ all. Peace on earth good _

will to men is the great - est gift of ___ all. ___

Happy Christmas, Little Friend

Lyrics by Oscar Hammerstein II
Music by Richard Rodgers

*Strum Pattern: 4
*Pick Pattern: 3

Verse
Moderately

The soft morn-ing light of a pale win-ter sun is trac-ing the trees on the snow, leap

*Use Pattern 8 for 2/4 meas.

up lit-tle friend and fly down the stairs for Christ-mas is wait-ing be-low. There's a

tree in the room run-ning o-ver with stars that twin-kle and sing to your eyes and

un-der the tree there are pres-ents that say un-wrap me and get a sur-

Chorus

prise. ____ Hap-py Christ-mas

lit-tle friend, may your heart be laugh-ing ____ all day. ____

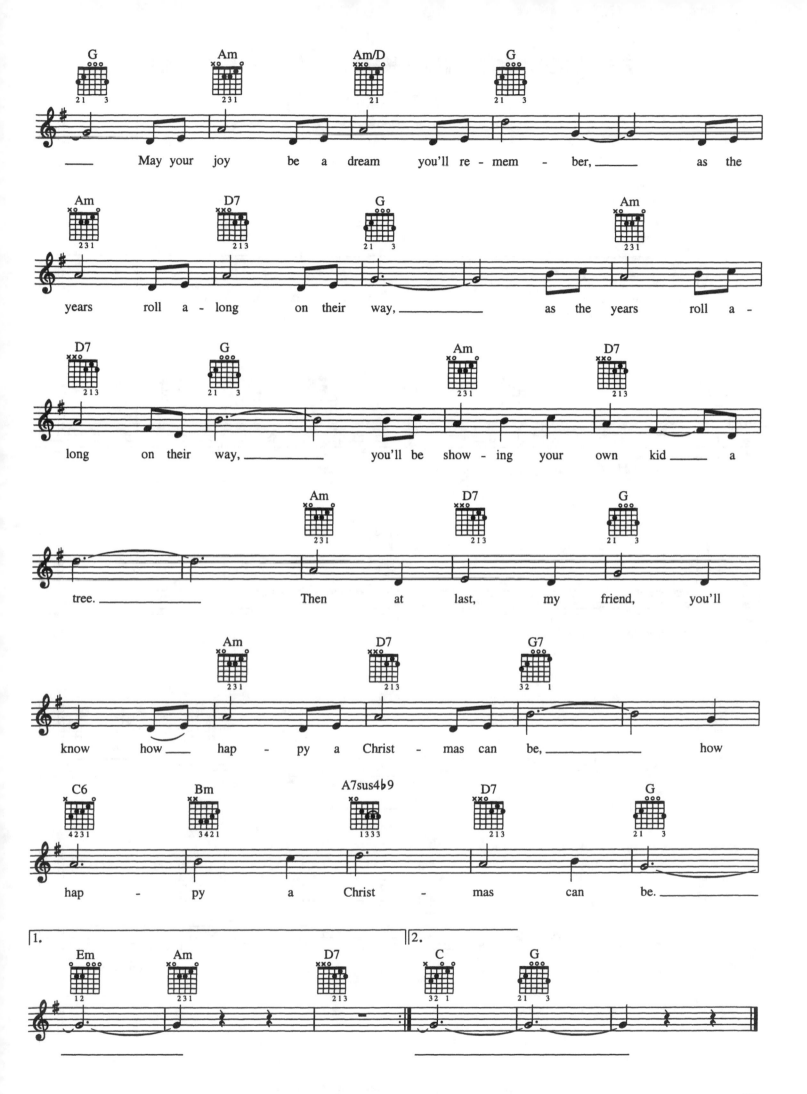

Happy Hanukkah, My Friend
(The Hanukkah Song)

Words and Music by Justin Wilde and Douglas Alan Konecky

Strum Pattern: 2
Pick Pattern: 2

Verse
Moderately

1. Spin the drei-del, light the lights, ev-'ry-one stay home to-night. The
2. *See Additional Lyrics*

sto-ry is told, __ the young and the old __ to-geth - er. As

twi-light greets the set-ting sun, light the can-dles one by one. Re -

mem-ber the past, __ tra-di-tions that last __ for - ev - er.

Chorus

Come, let's share the joy of Ha - nuk - kah. May our friend-ship grow. __

Additional Lyrics

2. Candlelight or star above,
   Messages of peace and love;
   Their meaning is clear, we all were put here as brothers.
   So let's begin with you and me,
   Let friendship shine eternally,
   May this holiday enlighten the way for others.

Happy Holiday

from the Motion Picture Irving Berlin's HOLIDAY INN

Words and Music by Irving Berlin

Strum Pattern: 3, 2
Pick Pattern: 3, 4

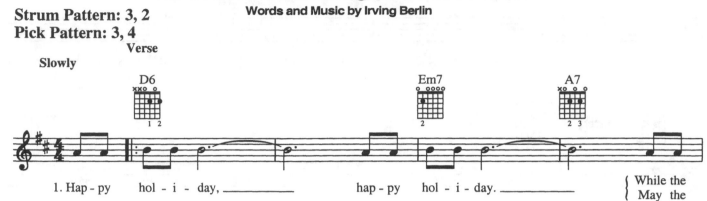

1. Hap-py hol-i-day, _____ hap-py hol-i-day. _____

{ While the
{ May the

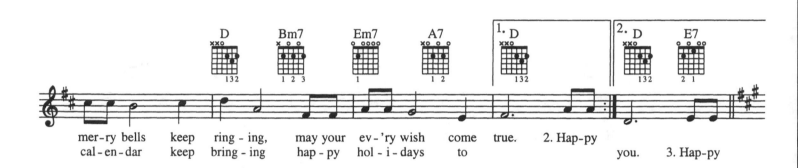

mer-ry bells keep ring-ing, may your ev-'ry wish come true. 2. Hap-py .... you. 3. Hap-py
cal-en-dar keep bring-ing hap-py hol-i-days to

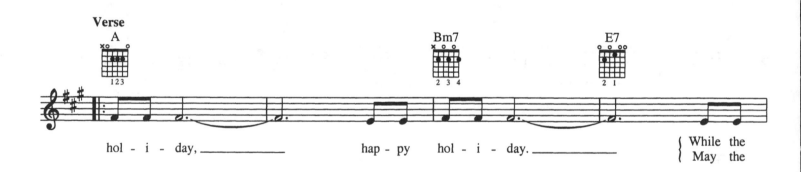

hol-i-day, _____ hap-py hol-i-day. _____

{ While the
{ May the

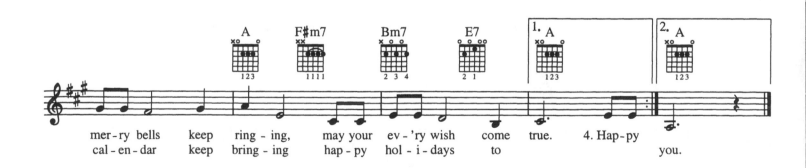

mer-ry bells keep ring-ing, may your ev-'ry wish come true. 4. Hap-py .... you.
cal-en-dar keep bring-ing hap-py hol-i-days to

Happy New Year Darling

Music and Lyrics by Carmen Lombardo and Johnny Marks

Happy Xmas (War Is Over)

Words and Music by John Lennon and Yoko Ono

Strum Pattern: 8
Pick Pattern: 8

Hark! The Herald Angels Sing

Words by Charles Wesley
Altered by George Whitefield
Music by Felix Mendelssohn-Bartholdy
Arranged by William H. Cummings

Strum Pattern: 2, 3
Pick Pattern: 3, 4

Verse
Joyfully

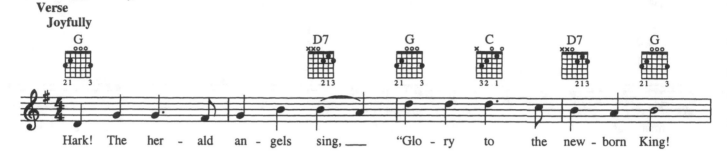

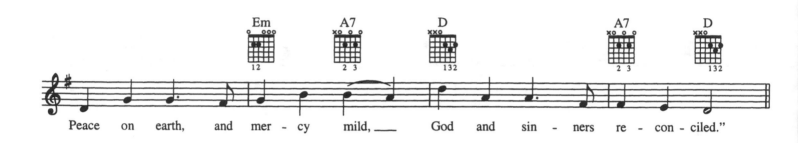

Hark! The her - ald an - gels sing, ___ "Glo - ry to the new - born King!

Peace on earth, and mer - cy mild, ___ God and sin - ners re - con - ciled."

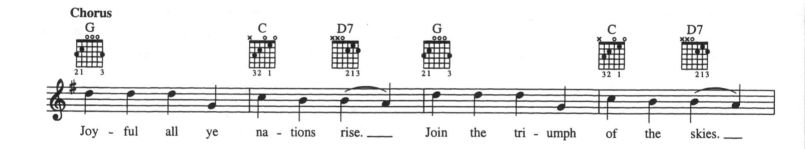

Chorus

Joy - ful all ye na - tions rise. ___ Join the tri - umph of the skies. ___

With th'an - gel - ic host pro - claim, "Christ is ___ born in Beth - le - hem."

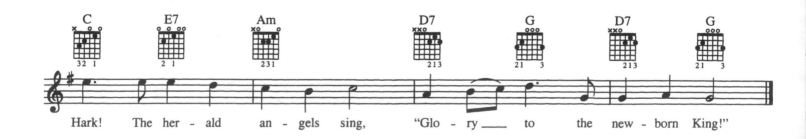

Hark! The her - ald an - gels sing, "Glo - ry ___ to the new - born King!"

He

Words Richard Mullen
Music by Jack Richards

Strum Pattern: 9
Pick Pattern: 9

Intro
Moderately Slow

1. He can turn the tides and calm the an-gry sea. He a-lone de-cides who writes a sym-pho-ny. He lights ev-'ry star that makes our dark-ness bright. He keeps watch all through each long and lone-ly night. He still finds the time to hear a child's first prayer. Saint or sin-ner, call and al-ways find Him there.

2. *See Additional Lyrics*

Chorus

Though it makes him sad to see the way we live, he'll al-ways say,

"I for- give."

give, I for- give."

Additional Lyrics

2. He can grant a wish or make a dream come true.
He can paint the clouds and turn the gray to blue.
He alone knows where to find the rainbow's end.
He alone can see what lies beyond the bend.
He can touch a tree and turn the leaves to gold.
He knows every lie that you and I have told.

Hear Them Bells

Words and Music by D.S. McCosh

Strum Pattern: 3
Pick Pattern: 3

Verse
Brightly

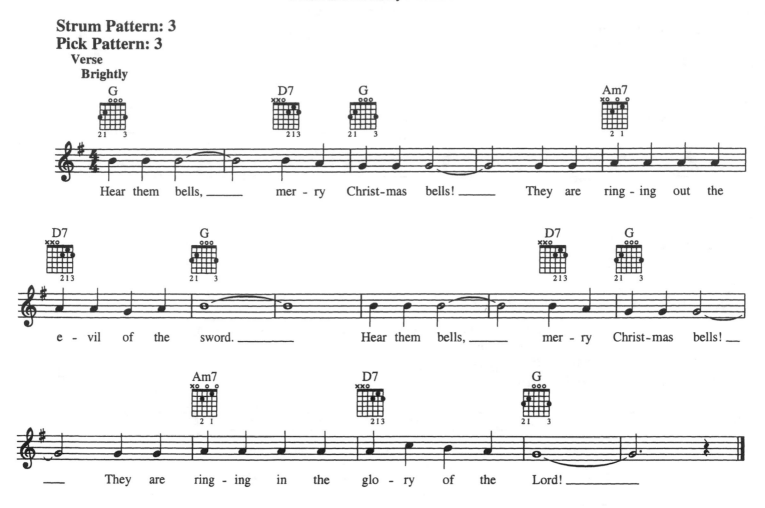

Hear them bells, _____ mer - ry Christ-mas bells! _____ They are ring - ing out the

e - vil of the sword. _____ Hear them bells, _____ mer - ry Christ-mas bells! _

_ They are ring - ing in the glo - ry of the Lord! _____

A Holly Jolly Christmas

Music and Lyrics by Johnny Marks

Strum Pattern: 2, 3
Pick Pattern: 3, 4

Verse
Brightly

1. Have a hol - ly jol - ly Christ-mas, it's the best time of the year.

Here We Come A-Wassailing

Traditional

Strum Pattern: 7, 9
Pick Pattern: 7, 9

Strum Pattern: 3
Pick Pattern: 3

Additional Lyrics

2. We are not daily beggars
   That beg from door to door.
   But we are neighbor children
   Whom you have seen before.

3. We have got a little purse
   Of stretching leather skin.
   We want a little money
   To line it well within:

4. God bless the master of this house,
   Likewise the mistress too;
   And all the little children
   That round the table go:

The Holly and the Ivy

18th Century English Carol

Strum Pattern: 8
Pick Pattern: 8

Verse
Moderately Slow

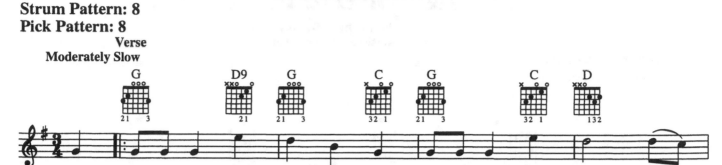

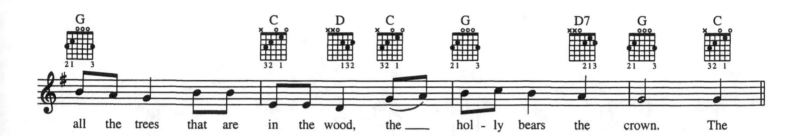

1. The hol - ly and the i - vy, when they are both full grown, of ___
2., 3. *See Additional Lyrics*

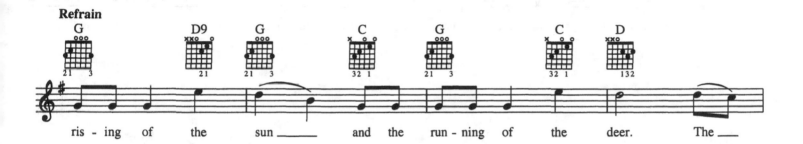

all the trees that are in the wood, the ___ hol - ly bears the crown. The

Refrain

ris - ing of the sun ___ and the run - ning of the deer. The ___

play - ing of the mer - ry or - gan, sweet sing - ing of the choir. 2., 3. The choir.

Additional Lyrics

2. The holly bears a blossom,
   As white as lily flow'r,
   And Mary bore sweet Jesus Christ,
   To be our sweet Saviour.

3. The holly bears a berry,
   As red as any blood,
   And Mary bore sweet Jesus Christ,
   To do poor sinners good.

(There's No Place Like)
Home for the Holidays

Words by Al Stillman
Music by Robert Allen

Strum Pattern: 3
Pick Pattern: 3

Chorus

Moderately

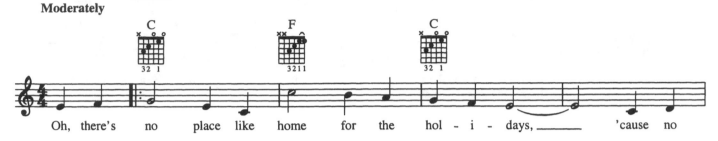

Oh, there's no place like home for the hol - i - days, _____ 'cause no

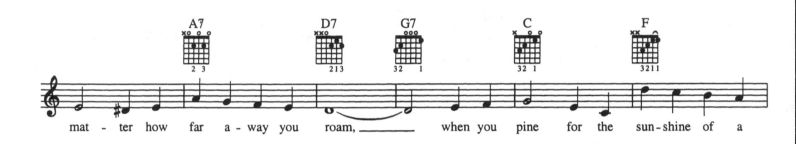

mat - ter how far a - way you roam, _____ when you pine for the sun - shine of a

friend - ly gaze, _____ for the hol - i - days you can't beat home, sweet home.

1. I met a
2. A home that

Verse

man who lives in Ten - nes - see and he was head - in' for Penn - syl - van - ia and some
knows your joy and laugh - ter filled with mem' - ries by the score is a home you're glad to

How Brightly Beams the Morning Star

Words and Music by Philipp Nicolai
Translated by William Mercer
Harmonized by J.S. Bach

Strum Pattern: 4
Pick Pattern: 3

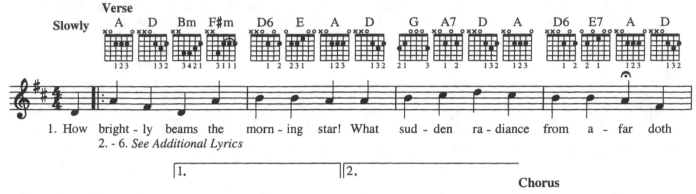

Verse

Slowly

1. How bright - ly beams the morn - ing star! What sud - den ra - diance from a - far doth
2. - 6. *See Additional Lyrics*

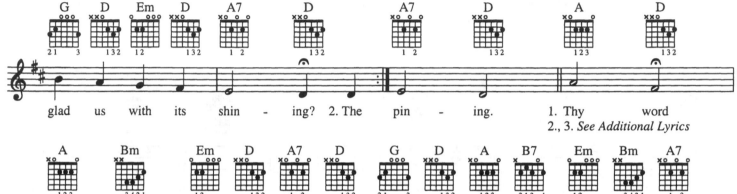

glad us with its shin - ing? 2. The pin - ing. 1. Thy word
2., 3. *See Additional Lyrics*

Chorus

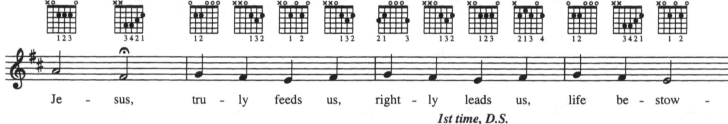

Je - sus, tru - ly feeds us, right - ly leads us, life be - stow -

1st time, D.S.
(take repeat)
2nd time, D.S. al Coda
(take repeat)

To Coda ⊕

⊕ Coda

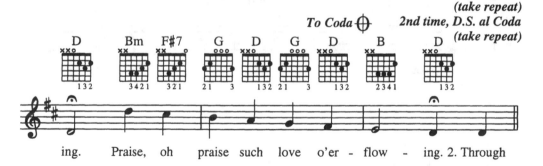

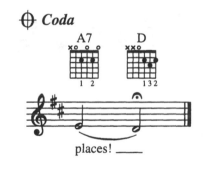

ing. Praise, oh praise such love o'er - flow - ing. 2. Through

places! ____

Additional Lyrics

2. The ray of God that breaks our night.
   And fills the darkened souls with light,
   Who long for truth were pining.

3. Through thee alone can we be blest;
   Then deep be on our hearts imprest
   The love that thou hast borne us.

4. So make us ready to fulfill
   With burning zeal thy holy will,
   Though men may vex or scorn us.

Chorus 2. Saviour, let us never lose thee,
   For we choose thee,
   Thirst to know thee
   All we are and have we owe thee!

5. O praise to him who came to save,
   Who conquer'd death and burst the grave.
   Each day new praise resoundeth.

6. To him the Lamb who once was slain,
   The friend whom none shall trust in vain,
   Whose grace for ay aboundeth.

Chorus 3. Sing, ye heavens, tell the story
   Of his glory,
   Till his praises
   Flood with light earth's darkest places!

How Lovely Is Christmas

Words by Arnold Sundgaard
Music by Alec Wilder

Strum Pattern: 7
Pick Pattern: 7

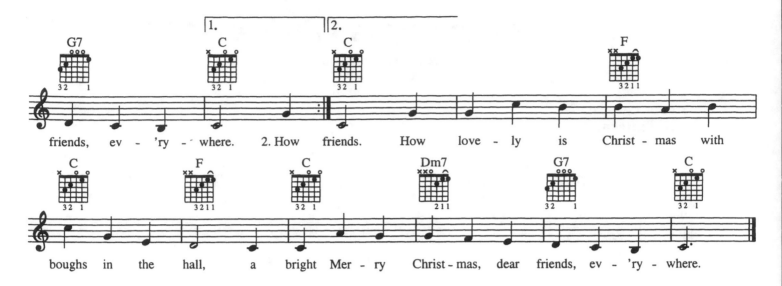

friends, ev - 'ry - where. 2. How friends. How love - ly is Christ - mas with
boughs in the hall, a bright Mer - ry Christ - mas, dear friends, ev - 'ry - where.

Additional Lyrics

2. How lovely is Christmas when children are near,
The sound of their laughter, sweet season of cheer.
How lovely is Christmas with gifts by the tree,
Each gift tells a story, oh, what will it be.
The Yule Log is burning, the stars gleam above;
Remember the gift of the Christ Child is love.
The bells ring for Christmas, our story now ends.
Goodnight, Merry Christmas, dear neighbors and friends.
How lovely is Christmas with boughs in the hall,
A bright Merry Christmas, dear friends, ev'rywhere.

I Still Believe in Santa Claus

Words and Music by Maurice Starr and Al Lancellotti

*Strum Pattern: 4
*Pick Pattern: 3

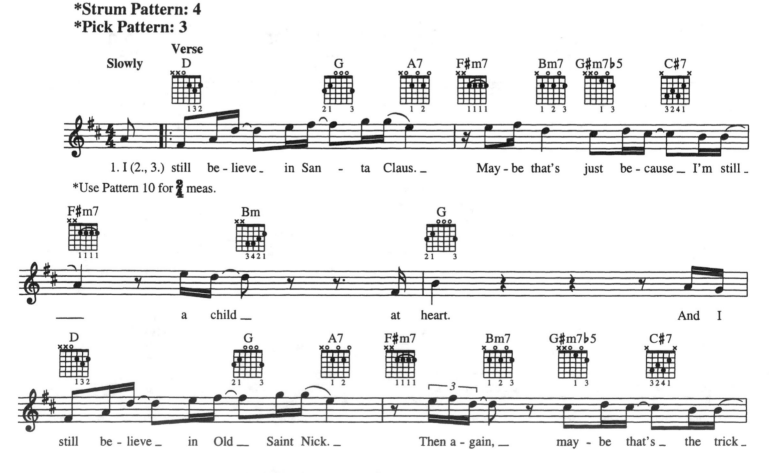

1. I (2., 3.) still be - lieve _ in San - ta Claus. _ May - be that's just be - cause _ I'm still _

*Use Pattern 10 for ⅔ meas.

____ a child ____ at heart. And I

still be - lieve _ in Old _ Saint Nick. _ Then a - gain, _ may - be that's _ the trick _

Hymne

By Vangelis

Strum Pattern: 9
Pick Pattern: 9

I Heard the Bells on Christmas Day

Words by Henry Wadsworth Longfellow
Adapted by Johnny Marks
Music by Johnny Marks

Strum Pattern: 4
Pick Pattern: 5

Verse
Simply

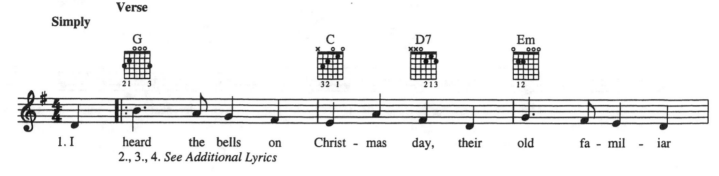

1. I heard the bells on Christ - mas day, their old fa - mil - iar
2., 3., 4. *See Additional Lyrics*

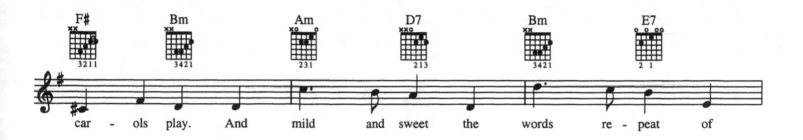

car - ols play. And mild and sweet the words re - peat of

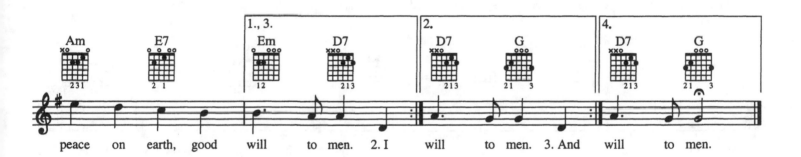

peace on earth, good will to men. | 2. I will to men. | 3. And will to men.

Additional Lyrics

2. I thought as now this day had come,
   The belfries of all Christendom
   Had rung so long the unbroken song
   Of peace on earth, good will to men.

3. And in despair I bowed my head;
   "There is no peace on earth," I said,
   "For hate is strong, and mocks the song
   Of peace on earth, good will to men."

4. Then pealed the bells more loud and deep;
   "God is not dead, nor noth He sleep.
   The wrong shall fail, the right prevail
   With peace on earth good will to men."

I Saw Mommy Kissing Santa Claus

Words and Music by Tommie Connor

Strum Pattern: 2, 3
Pick Pattern: 3, 4

I Wonder As I Wander

By John Jacob Niles

Strum Pattern: 8
Pick Pattern: 8

Verse
Slowly

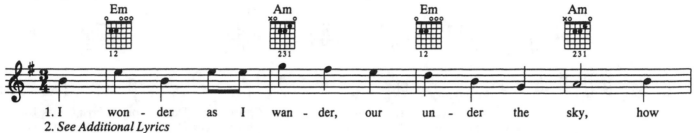

1. I won-der as I wan-der, our un-der the sky, how
2. *See Additional Lyrics*

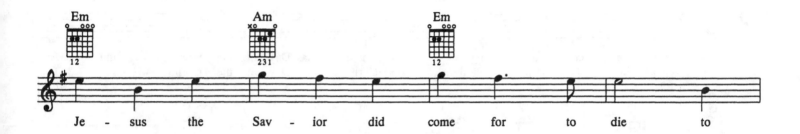

Je - sus the Sav - ior did come for to die to

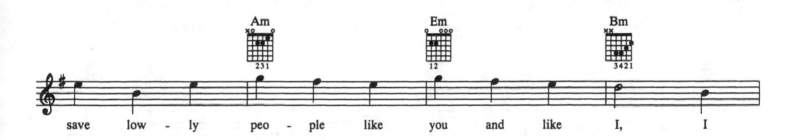

save low - ly peo - ple like you and like I, I

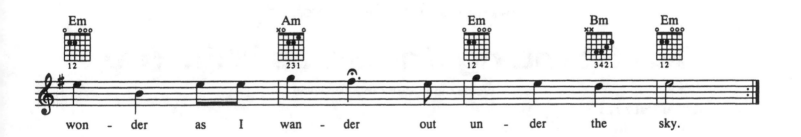

won - der as I wan - der out un - der the sky.

Additional Lyrics

2. When Jesus was born, it was in a cow's stall,
   With shepherds and wise men and angels and all.
   The blessings of Christmas from heaven did fall
   And the weary world woke to the Savior's call.

I Saw Three Ships

Traditional English Carol

Strum Pattern: 8, 7
Pick Pattern: 8, 9

Verse
Spirited

G D G D G D

1. I saw three ships come sail - ing in, on Christ - mas Day, on Christ - mas Day; I
   what was in those ships, all three, on Christ - mas Day, on Christ - mas Day; And

G D G D G D G

saw three ships come sail - ing in, on Christ - mas Day in the morn - ing. 2. And
what was in those ships, all three, on Christ - mas Day in the morn - ing. 3. The

Verse

G D G D G D

Vir - gin Mar - y and Christ were there, on Christ - mas Day, on Christ - mas Day; The

G D G D G D G

Vir - gin Mar - y and Christ were there, on Christ - mas Day in the morn - ing.

I'm Spending Christmas With You

Words and Music by Tom Occhipinti

Strum Pattern: 7
Pick Pattern: 7

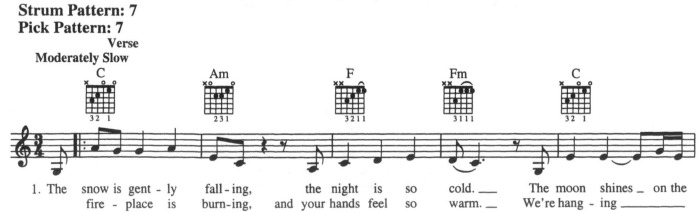

Verse
Moderately Slow

C Am F Fm C

1. The snow is gent - ly fall - ing, the night is so cold. ___ The moon shines ___ on the
   fire - place is burn - ing, and your hands feel so warm. ___ We're hang - ing _____

I'll Be Home for Christmas

Words and Music by Kim Gannon and Walter Kent

Strum Pattern: 4, 3
Pick Pattern: 4, 3

In the Field With Their Flocks Abiding

Traditional

Strum Pattern: 4
Pick Pattern: 3
Verse
Moderately

In the field with their flocks a - bid - ing, they lay on the dew - y ground. And

glim - mer - ing un - der the star - light, the sheep lay white a - round. When the

light of the Lord streamed o'er them, and lo! from the heav - en a - bove, an

an - gel leaned from the glo - ry, and sang his song of love. He

sang that first sweet Christ - mas the song that shall nev - er cease,

"Glo - ry to God in the high - est, on earth good will and peace."

Infant Holy, Infant Lowly

Traditional Polish Carol
Paraphrased by Edith M.G. Reed

Strum Pattern: 7, 9
Pick Pattern: 7, 9

Verse
Lyrically

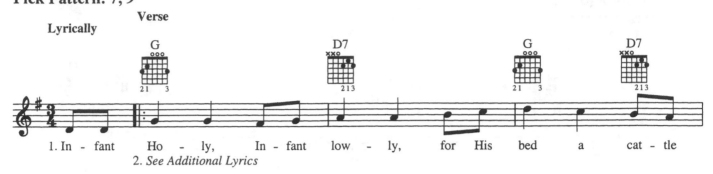

1. In - fant Ho - ly, In - fant low - ly, for His bed a cat - tle
2. *See Additional Lyrics*

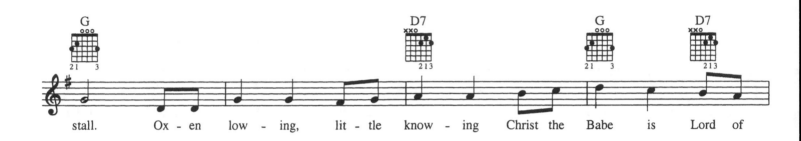

stall. Ox - en low - ing, lit - tle know - ing Christ the Babe is Lord of

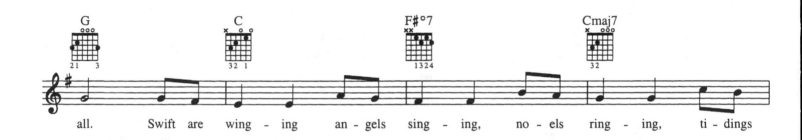

all. Swift are wing - ing an - gels sing - ing, no - els ring - ing, ti - dings

bring - ing: Christ the Babe is Lord of all! Flocks are you. _____

Additional Lyrics

2. Flocks are sleeping, shepherds keeping
   Vigil 'til the morning new.
   Saw the glory, heard the story,
   Tidings of a Gospel true.
   Thus rejoicing, free from sorrow,
   Praises voicing, greet the morrow:
   Christ the Babe was born for you.

It Came Upon the Midnight Clear

Words by Edmund H. Sears
Traditional English Melody
Adapted by Arthur Sullivan

Strum Pattern: 8, 7
Pick Pattern: 8, 9

It Must Have Been the Mistletoe
(Our First Christmas)

By Doug Konecky and Justin Wilde

had his fin - gers crossed, that we would fall in love. ___ 2. It

Verse

could have been ___ the hol - i - day, ___ the mid-night ride ___ up - on a sleigh, ___ the

coun - try - side ___ all dressed in white, ___ that cra - zy snow - ball fight. It

could have been ___ the stee - ple bell ___ that wrapped us up with - in it's spell. ___ It

on - ly took one kiss to know, ___ it must have been the

Bridge

mis - tle - toe. Our first Christ - mas,

more than ___ we'd been dream - ing of. ___ Old Saint

Nich - 'las must have known that kiss would lead to all of this. ___ It

Outro

must have been ___ the mis - tle - toe, ___ the la - zy fire, ___ the fall - ing snow, _ the

mag - ic in ___ the frost - y air, ___ that made me love you. On

Christ - mas Eve ___ a wish come true, ___ that night I ___ fell in love with you. ___ It

on - ly took ___ one kiss to know, _ it must have been the

mis - tle - toe! It must have been the mis - tle - toe! It

must have been the mis - tle - toe!

Jesu, Joy of Man's Desiring

By Johann Sebastian Bach

Strum Pattern: 8
Pick Pattern: 8

Intro
Moderately

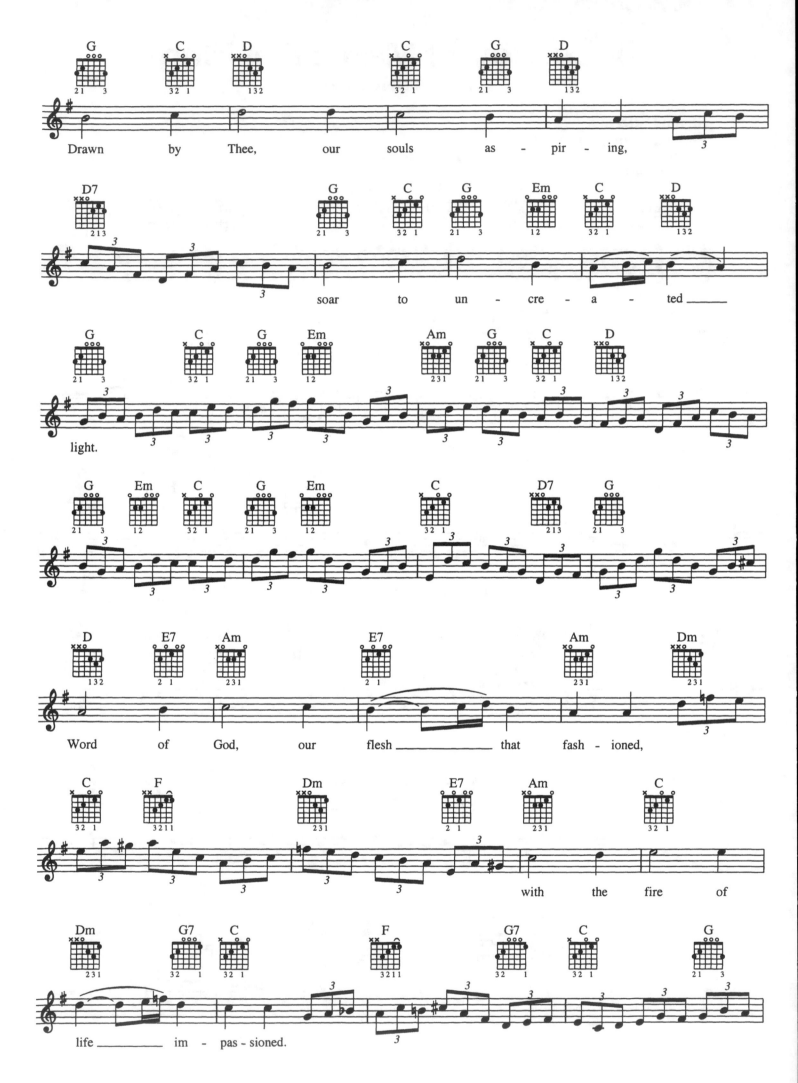

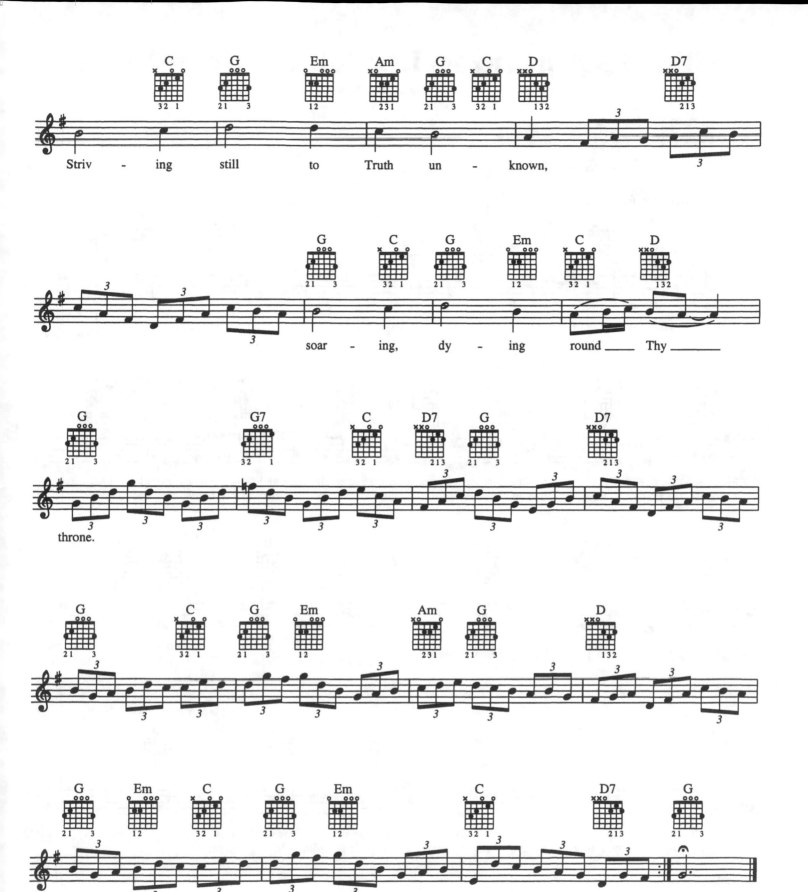

Additional Lyrics

2. Through the way where hope is guiding.
Hark, what peaceful music rings!
Where the flock in Thee confiding,
Drink of joy from deathless springs.
Their's is beauty's fairest pleasure.
Their's is wisdom's holiest treasure.
Thou dost ever lead Thine own,
In the love of joys unknown.

It's Beginning to Look Like Christmas

By Meredith Willson

Strum Pattern: 2, 3
Pick Pattern: 3, 4

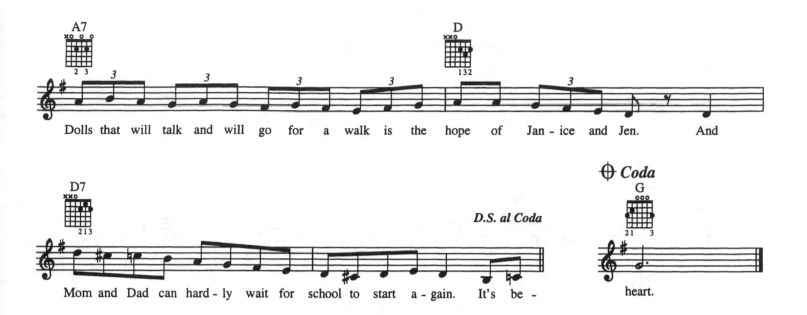

Dolls that will talk and will go for a walk is the hope of Jan-ice and Jen. And

D.S. al Coda

Mom and Dad can hard-ly wait for school to start a-gain. It's be-

Coda

heart.

It's Christmas Time All Over the World

Words and Music by Hugh Martin

Strum Pattern: 4
Pick Pattern: 3

1. It's (3.) Christ - mas time all o - ver the world, ___ and
2., 4. *See Additional Lyrics*

Christ - mas here at home. _____ The

church bells chime wher - ev - er we roam, ___ so

Joy - eux No - ël, Fe - liz Na - tal,
(Zhwah - yuh No - el) (Feh - leez Nah - tahl)

Joy - eux   No - ël,   Fe - liz   Na - tal,
(Zhwah - yuh   No - el)   (Feh - leez   Nah - tahl)

Gel - luk - kig Kerst - feest   to   you! _____
(Huh - lukh - kuh Kairst - feest)

1. _____ **2.** _____

2., 4. The _____   Though the

Bridge

cus - toms _____ may   change, _____   and the   lan - guage _____

_____ is   strange, _____   this ap - peal we   feel   is

real   in   Hol - land   or   Hong _____   Kong. _____   It's

Outro

Christ - mas   time   all   o - ver   the   world, _____   in

118

Additional Lyrics

2., 4. The snow is thick in most of the world
And children's eyes are wide
As old Saint Nick gets ready to ride,
So Feliz Navidad, Crăciun Fericit,
(Feh-lees Nah-vee-dahd) (Krah-choon Feeh-ree-cheet)
And Happy New Year to you!

It's Christmas in New York

Words and Music by Billy Butt

Interlude

Outro

Additional Lyrics

2. Rest'rant signs swaying, blue skies are graying,
   Ev'ryone saying, it's Christmas in New York.
   Skyscrapers gleaming, Broadway lights beaming,
   Children are dreaming, it's Christmas in New York.

Bridge The lights on the Christmas tree are fine,
   The sights of shopping sprees, the gifts, yours and mine.

It's Just Another New Year's Eve

Lyric by Marty Panzer
Music by Barry Manilow

Strum Pattern: 6
Pick Pattern: 3

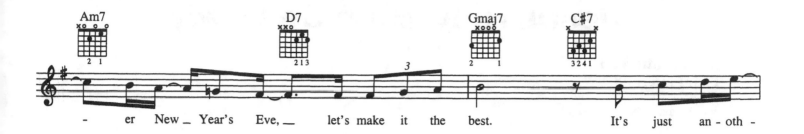

- er New _ Year's Eve, _ let's make it the best. It's just an - oth -

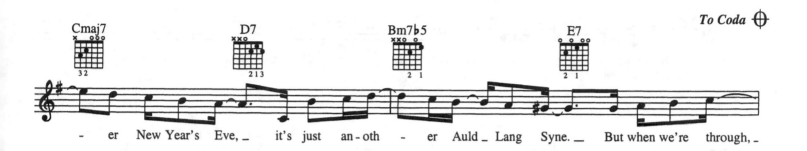

To Coda ⊕

- er New Year's Eve, _ it's just an - oth - er Auld _ Lang Syne. _ But when we're through, _

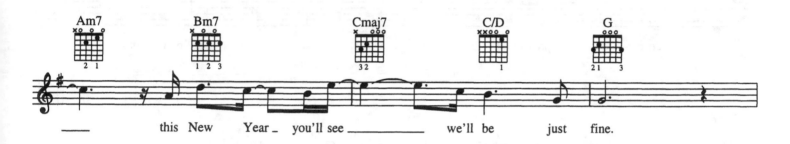

_ this New Year _ you'll see _____ we'll be just fine.

D.S. al Coda
(take 2nd ending)

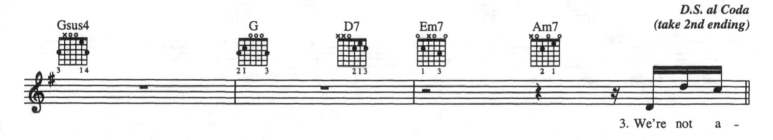

3. We're not a -

⊕ *Coda*

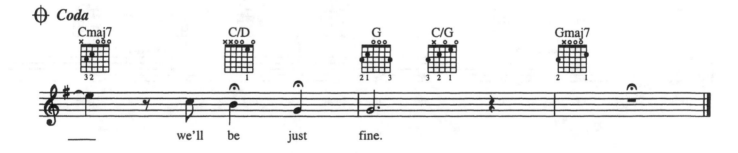

_ we'll be just fine.

Additional Lyrics

2. We've made mistakes but we've made good friends, too.
   Remember all the nights we've spent with them and all our plans.
   Who says they can't come true?
   Tonight's another chance to start again.

3. We're not alone, we've got the world, you know.
   And it won't let us down, just wait and see.
   And we'll grow old, but think how wise we'll grow,
   There's more you know, it's only New Year's Eve.

Jesus Holy, Born So Lowly

Traditional Polish

Strum Pattern: 8
Pick Pattern: 8

Verse
Moderately

1. Je - sus ho - ly, born so low - ly, we still sing you car - ols gay.
2. *See Additional Lyrics*

Je - sus dear - est, pre - cious in - fant, come to us from heav'n to - day.

Chorus

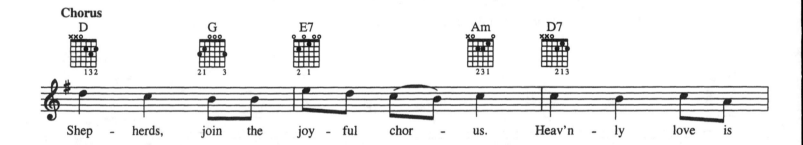

Shep - herds, join the joy - ful chor - us. Heav'n - ly love is

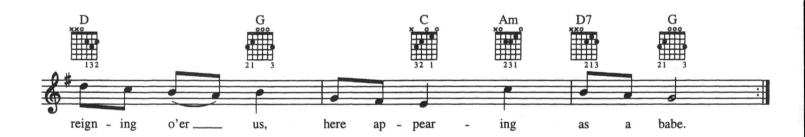

reign - ing o'er ___ us, here ap - pear - ing as a babe.

Additional Lyrics

2. On the straw the Babe is sleeping,
   In the humble manger bed.
   Mary loving watch is keeping,
   Angels hover 'round His head.
   Shepherds bow in adoration,
   Praising God's sweet benediction
   That upon the earth is shed.

Jingle-Bell Rock

Words and Music by Joe Beal and Jim Boothe

Strum Pattern: 1, 3
Pick Pattern: 2, 3

Verse
Moderate Rock

Jingle, Jingle, Jingle

Music and Lyrics by Johnny Marks

Strum Pattern: 4
Pick Pattern: 4

Verse
Moderately

Jingle Bells

Words and Music by J. Pierpont

Strum Pattern: 2, 3
Pick Pattern: 3, 4

Additional Lyrics

2. A day or two ago, I thought I'd take a ride,
And soon Miss Fannie Bright was sitting by my side.
The horse was lean and lank,
Misfortune seemed his lot.
He got into a drifted bank and we, we got upshot! Oh!

3. Now the ground is white, go it while you're young.
Take the girls tonight and sing this sleighing song.
Just get a bobtail bay,
Two-forty for his speed.
Then hitch him to an open sleigh and
Crack, you'll take the lead! Oh

Jolly Old St. Nicholas

Traditional 19th Century American Carol

Strum Pattern: 10
Pick Pattern: 10

Verse
Brightly

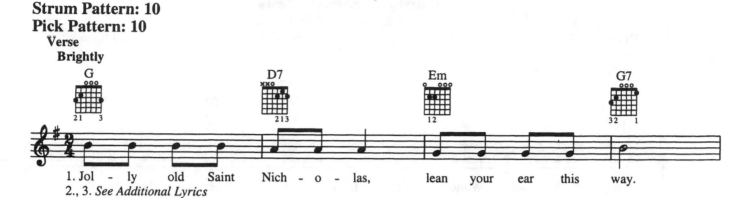

1. Jol - ly old Saint Nich - o - las, lean your ear this way.
2., 3. *See Additional Lyrics*

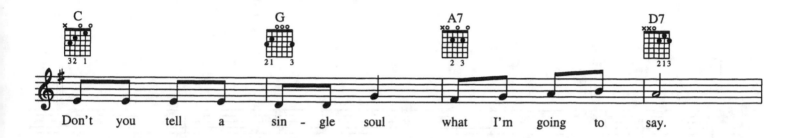

Don't you tell a sin - gle soul what I'm going to say.

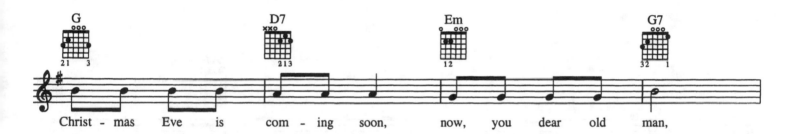

Christ - mas Eve is com - ing soon, now, you dear old man,

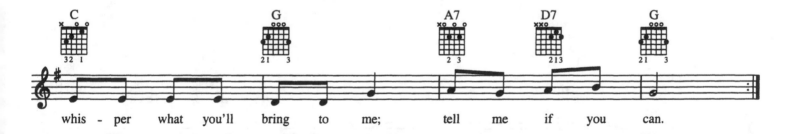

whis - per what you'll bring to me; tell me if you can.

Additional Lyrics

2. When the clock is striking twelve, when I'm fast asleep.
   Down the chimney broad and black, with your pack you'll creep.
   All the stockings you will find hanging in a row.
   Mine will be the shortest one, you'll be sure to know.

3. Johnny wants a pair of skates; Susy wants a sled.
   Nellie wants a picture book, yellow, blue and red.
   Now I think I'll leave to you what to give the rest.
   Choose for me, dear Santa Claus.
   You will know the best.

Joy to the World

Words by Isaac Watts
Music by George Frideric Handel
Arranged by Lowell Mason

Strum Pattern: 3
Pick Pattern: 3
Verse
With Spirit

1. Joy to the World! The Lord is come: Let earth re-
2. *See Additional Lyrics*

ceive her King. Let ev - 'ry ___ heart ___ pre - pare ___ Him ___

room. ___ And heav - en and na - ture ___ sing. And ___ heav - en and na - ture ___

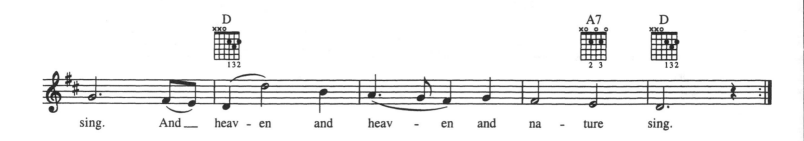

sing. And ___ heav - en and heav - en and na - ture sing.

Additional Lyrics

2. He rules the world with truth and grace
   And makes the nations prove
   The glories of His righteousness
   And wonders of His love,
   And wonders of His love.
   And wonders, wonders of His love.

Joyous Christmas

Music and Lyrics by Johnny Marks

Strum Pattern: 4
Pick Pattern: 3

Additional Lyrics

2. Have a Joyous Christmas, Joyous Christmas,
   But don't fail to recall
   That a tiny stranger
   In a manger was the start of it all.

3. Have a Joyous Christmas, Joyous Christmas,
   Sing it loudly and then
   Pray to all your worth for peace
   On earth and for good will to men.

Last Christmas

Words and Music by George Michael

Strum Pattern: 6
Pick Pattern: 3

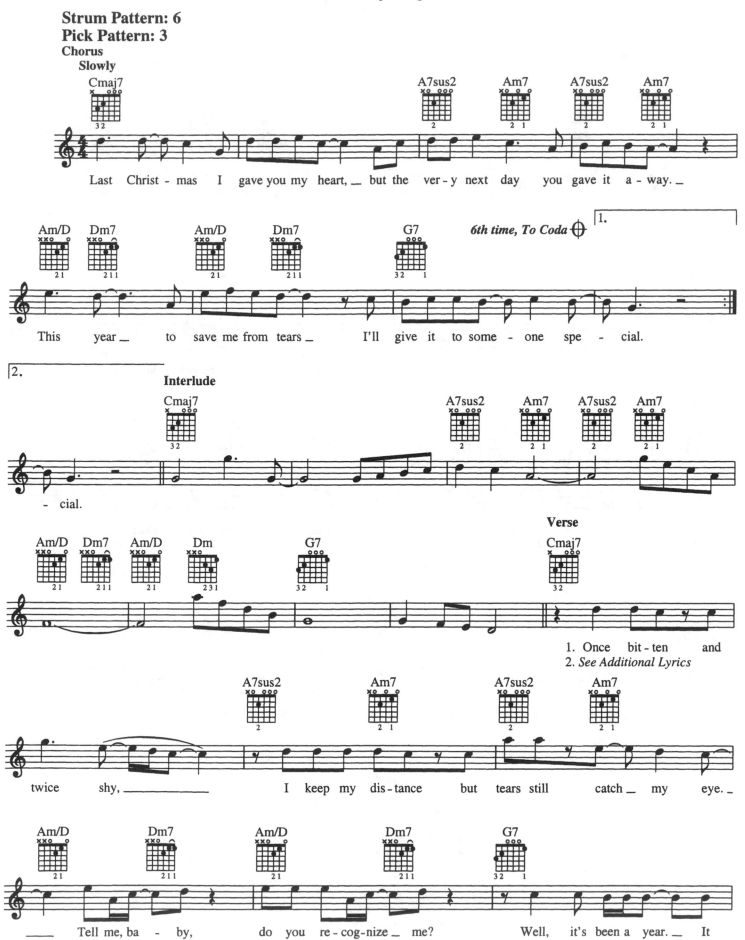

Last Christmas I gave you my heart, __ but the ver-y next day you gave it a-way. __

This year __ to save me from tears __ I'll give it to some-one spe-cial.

-cial.

1. Once bit-ten and
2. *See Additional Lyrics*

twice shy, _____ I keep my dis-tance but tears still catch __ my eye. __

__ Tell me, ba-by, do you re-cog-nize __ me? Well, it's been a year. __ It

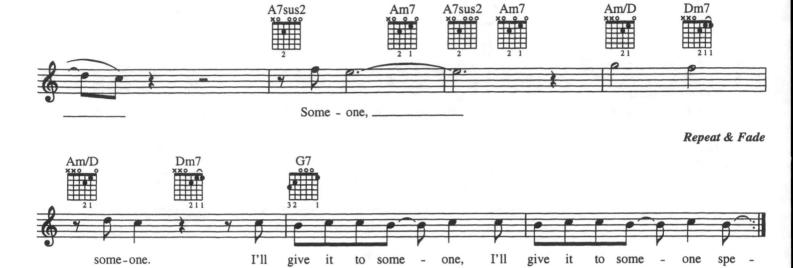

Some - one, _____

Repeat & Fade

some - one. I'll give it to some - one, I'll give it to some - one spe -

Additional Lyrics

2. A crowded room, friends with tired eyes.
   I'm hiding from you and your soul of ice.
   My God, I thought you were someone to rely on.
   Me, I guess I was a shoulder to cry on.
   A face on a lover with a fire in his heart,
   A man undercover but you tore me apart.
   Ooh, now I've found a real love.
   You'll never fool me again.

Let's Have an Old Fashioned Christmas

Lyric by Larry Conley
Music by Joe Solomon

Strum Pattern: 4
Pick Pattern: 3

Intro

Moderately

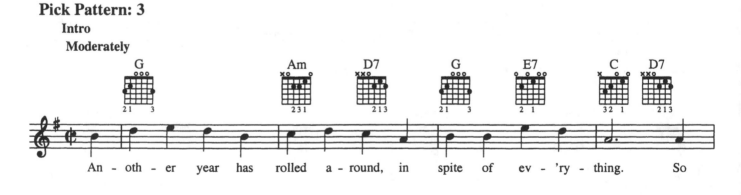

An - oth - er year has rolled a - round, in spite of ev - 'ry - thing. So

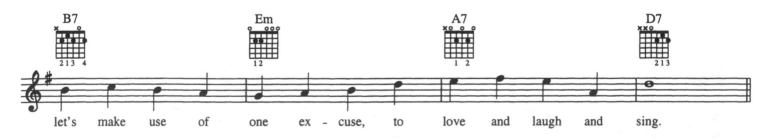

let's make use of one ex - cuse, to love and laugh and sing.

The Last Month of the Year
(What Month Was Jesus Born In?)

Words and Music by Vera Hall
Adapted and Arranged by Ruby Pickens Tartt and Alan Lomax

Strum Pattern: 6
Pick Pattern: 3

1. What month was my Je-sus born in? Last month of the year!
2. *See Additional Lyrics*

What month was my Je-sus born in? Last month of the year! Oh,

Chorus

Jan-u-ar-y, Feb-ru-ar-y, March,

A-pril, May, June, O Lord, You got Ju-ly, Aug-ust, Sep-tem-ber, Oct-

to-ber and-a No-vem-ber, on the twen-ty fifth day of De-cem-ber in the

1., 2., 3. last month of the year.

4. Last month of the year.

Additional Lyrics

2. Well, they laid Him in the manger,
Last month of the year!
Well, they laid Him in the manger,
Last month of the year!

3. Wrapped Him up in swaddling clothing,
Last month of the year!
Wrapped Him up in swaddling clothing,
Last month of the year!

4. He was born of the Virgin Mary,
Last month of the year!
He was born of the Virgin Mary,
Last month of the year!

Let It Snow! Let It Snow! Let It Snow!

Words by Sammy Cahn
Music by Jule Styne

Strum Pattern: 2
Pick Pattern: 4

Lo, How a Rose E'er Blooming

15th Century German Carol
Translated by Theodore Baker
Music from Alte Catholische Geistliche Kirchengesang

Strum Pattern: 3, 4
Pick Pattern: 4, 5
Verse
Hymn

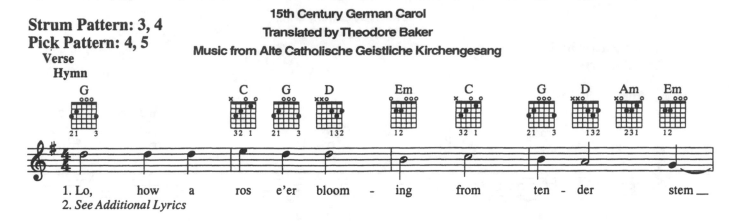

1. Lo, how a ros e'er bloom - ing from ten - der stem __
2. *See Additional Lyrics*

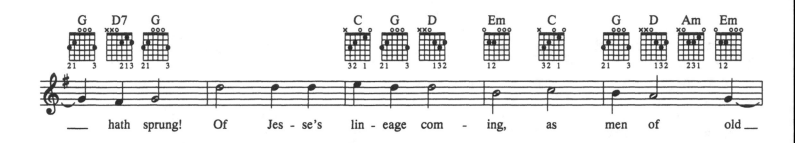

__ hath sprung! Of Jes - se's lin - eage com - ing, as men of old __

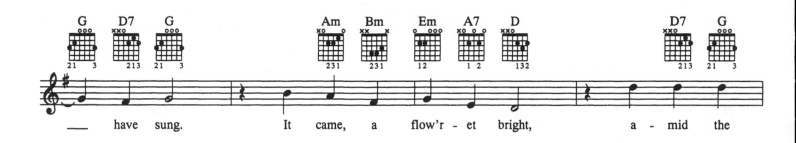

__ have sung. It came, a flow'r - et bright, a - mid the

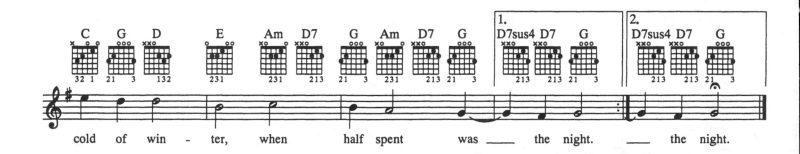

cold of win - ter, when half spent was __ the night. __ the night.

Additional Lyrics

2. Isaiah 'twas foretold it,
   The rose I have in mind.
   With Mary we behold it,
   The Virgin Mother kind.
   To show God's love aright.
   She bore to men a Savior
   When half spent was the night.

March of the Three Kings

Words by M.L. Hohman
Traditional French Melody

Strum Pattern: 10
Pick Pattern: 10

Chorus
March Tempo

A Marshmallow World

Words by Carl Sigman
Music by Peter De Rose

Strum Pattern: 3
Pick Pattern: 3

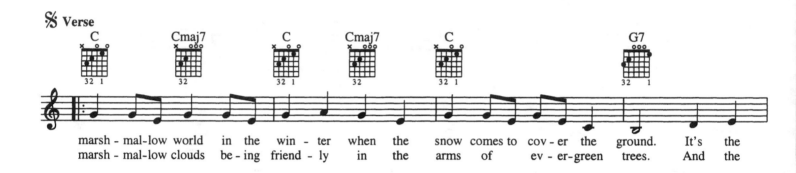

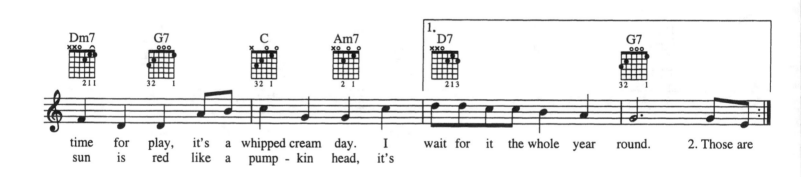

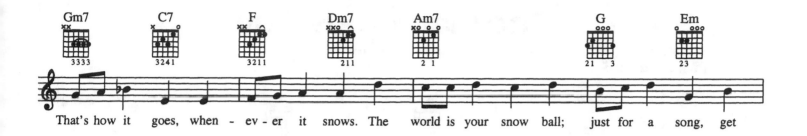

That's how it goes, when-ev-er it snows. The world is your snow ball; just for a song, get

Verse

out and roll it a - long. 3. It's a yum - yum-my world made for sweet hearts. Take a

walk with your fa - vor - ite girl. It's a su - gar date. What if spring is late? In

D.S. al Coda
(with repeat)   ⊕ *Coda*

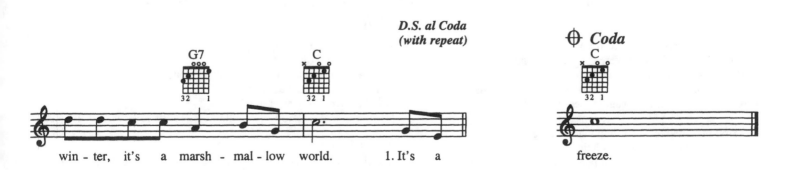

win - ter, it's a marsh - mal - low world. 1. It's a   freeze.

The Marvelous Toy

Strum Pattern: 3
Pick Pattern: 5

Words and Music by Tom Paxton

1. When I was just a wee lit-tle lad, full of health and joy, my
2., 3., 4. *See Additional Lyrics*

fa - ther home - ward came one night and gave to me a toy. A

won - der to be - hold it was, with man - y col - ors bright, and the mo - ment I laid

Chorus

eyes on it, it be - came my heart's de - light. It went "zip" when it moved, and

"bop" when it stopped, and "whirr" when it stood still. I nev - er knew just

1. - 4.

what it was and I guess I nev - er will. _____ 2. The will.

Additional Lyrics

2. The first time that I picked it up, I had a big surprise,
For right on its bottom were two big buttons
That looked like big green eyes.
I first pushed one and then the other, and then I twisted its lid,
And when I set it down again, here is what it did:

3. It first marched left and then marched right
And then marched under a chair,
And when I looked where it had gone, it wasn't even there!
I started to sob and my daddy laughed,
For he knew that I would find
When I turned around my marvelous toy, chugging from behind.

4. Well, the years have gone by too quickly, it seems,
And I have my own little boy.
And yesterday I gave to him my marvelous little toy.
His eyes nearly popped right out of his head,
And he gave a squeal of glee.
Neither one of us knows just what it is, but he loves it, just like me.

Final Chorus:
It still goes "zip" when it moves, and "bop" when it stops,
And "whirr" when it stands still.
I never knew just what it was,
And I guess I never will.

Mary Had a Baby

African-American Spiritual

Strum Pattern: 1, 3
Pick Pattern: 1, 3

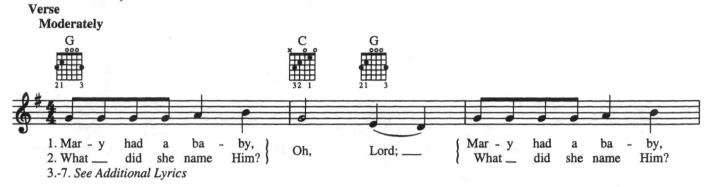

1. Mar - y had a ba - by,
2. What __ did she name Him? Oh, Lord; __ Mar - y had a ba - by, What __ did she name Him?
3.-7. *See Additional Lyrics*

Oh, my __ Lord; Mar - y had a ba - by, What __ did she name Him? Oh, Lord; __ The

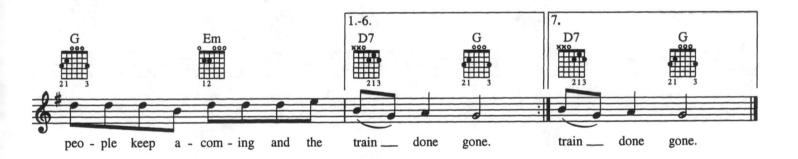

peo - ple keep a - com - ing and the train __ done gone. train __ done gone.

Additional Lyrics

3. She called Him Jesus,
4. Where was He born?
5. Born in a stable,
6. Where did they lay Him?
7. Laid Him in a manger,

Mary's Little Boy

Words and Music by Massie Patterson and Sammy Heyward

Strum Pattern: 4
Pick Pattern: 3

Verse
Moderately

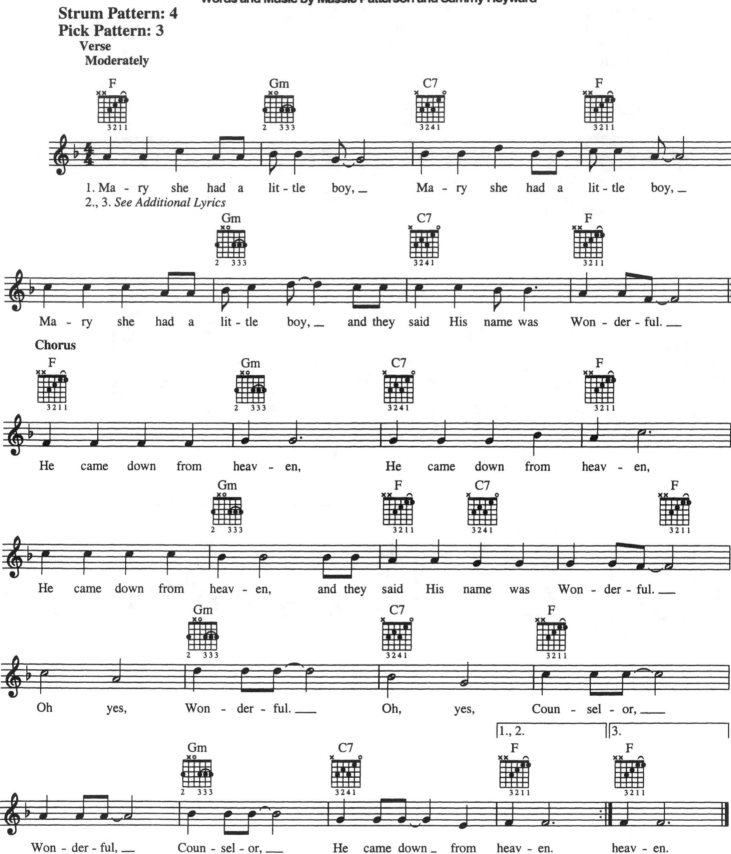

1. Ma - ry she had a lit - tle boy, __ Ma - ry she had a lit - tle boy, __
2., 3. *See Additional Lyrics*

Ma - ry she had a lit - tle boy, __ and they said His name was Won - der - ful. __

Chorus

He came down from heav - en, He came down from heav - en,

He came down from heav - en, and they said His name was Won - der - ful. __

Oh, yes, Won - der - ful. __ Oh, yes, Coun - sel - or, __

Won - der - ful, __ Coun - sel - or, __ He came down __ from heav - en. heav - en.

Additional Lyrics

2. Soldiers looked for the little boy,
Soldiers looked for the little boy,
Soldiers looked for the little boy,
And they said His name was Wonderful.

3. Wise men came running from the East,
Wise men came running from the East,
Wise men came running from the East,
And they said His name was Wonderful.

The Merry Christmas Polka

Words by Paul Francis Webster
Music by Sonny Burke

Strum Pattern: 4
Pick Pattern: 3

1. Come on and dance The Mer-ry Christ-mas Pol-ka, let ev-'ry-
   dance The Mer-ry Christ-mas Pol-ka, let ev-'ry

one be hap-py and gay. _____ Oh! It's the time to be
la - dy step with her beau _____ a-round a tree to the

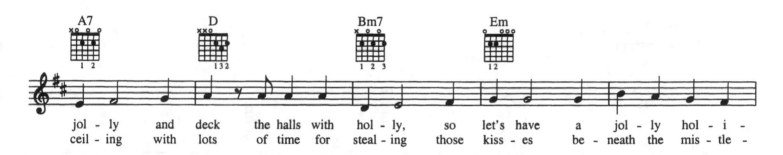

jol-ly and deck the halls with hol-ly, so let's have a jol-ly hol-i-
ceil-ing with lots of time for steal-ing those kiss-es be-neath the mis-tle-

day! _____ Come on and dance The Mer-ry Christ-mas Pol-ka,
toe! _____ Come on and dance The Mer-ry Christ-mas Pol-ka,

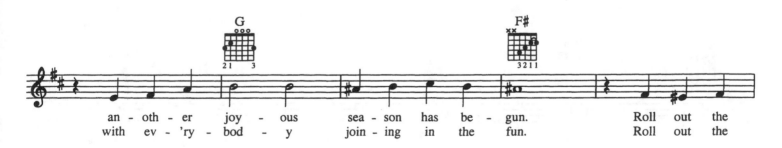

an-oth-er joy-ous sea-son has be-gun. Roll out the
with ev-'ry-bod-y join-ing in the fun. Roll out the

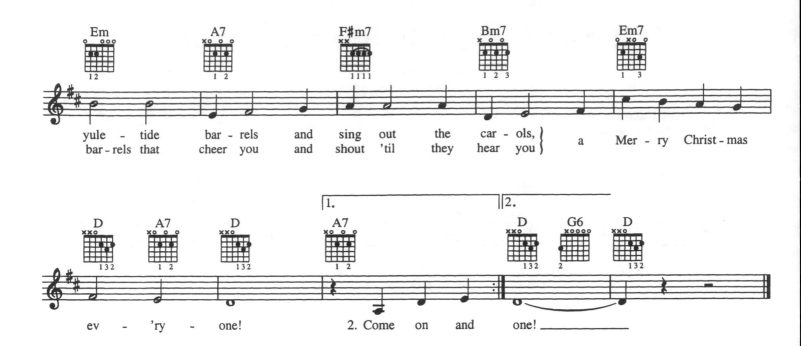

A Merry, Merry Christmas to You

Music and Lyrics by Johnny Marks

Strum Pattern: 8
Pick Pattern: 8

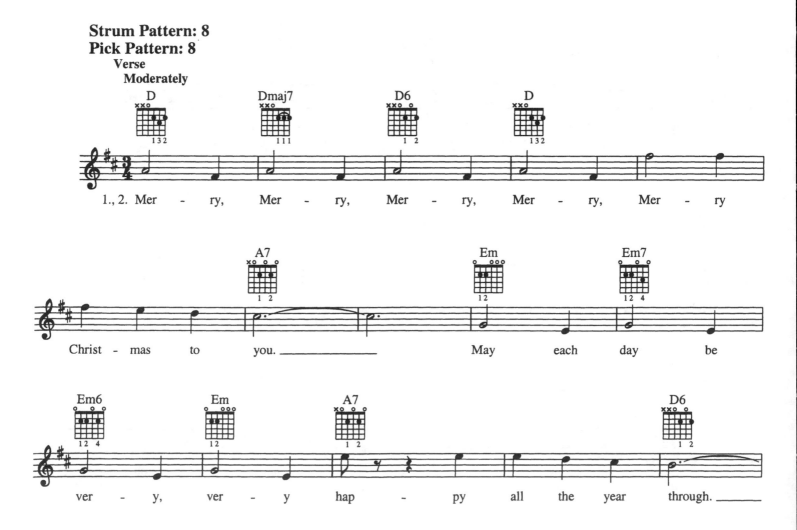

Merry Merry Christmas, Baby

Words and Music by Margo Sylvia and Gil Lopez

Strum Pattern: 8
Pick Pattern: 8

Intro
Moderately Slow

Verse

1. Mer-ry, mer-ry Christ-mas ba-by. _____ Al-though you're with some-bod-y new, _____ thought I'd send a card to hold _____ with-in my heart; _____ still grows though, we're _____ a-part. 2. Have a Mer-ry Christ-mas

Verse

ba-by, _____ and a Hap-py _ New Year too. _____ I am hop-ing that you'll met a hol-i-day I _ can't for-get 'cause that's when we fell in

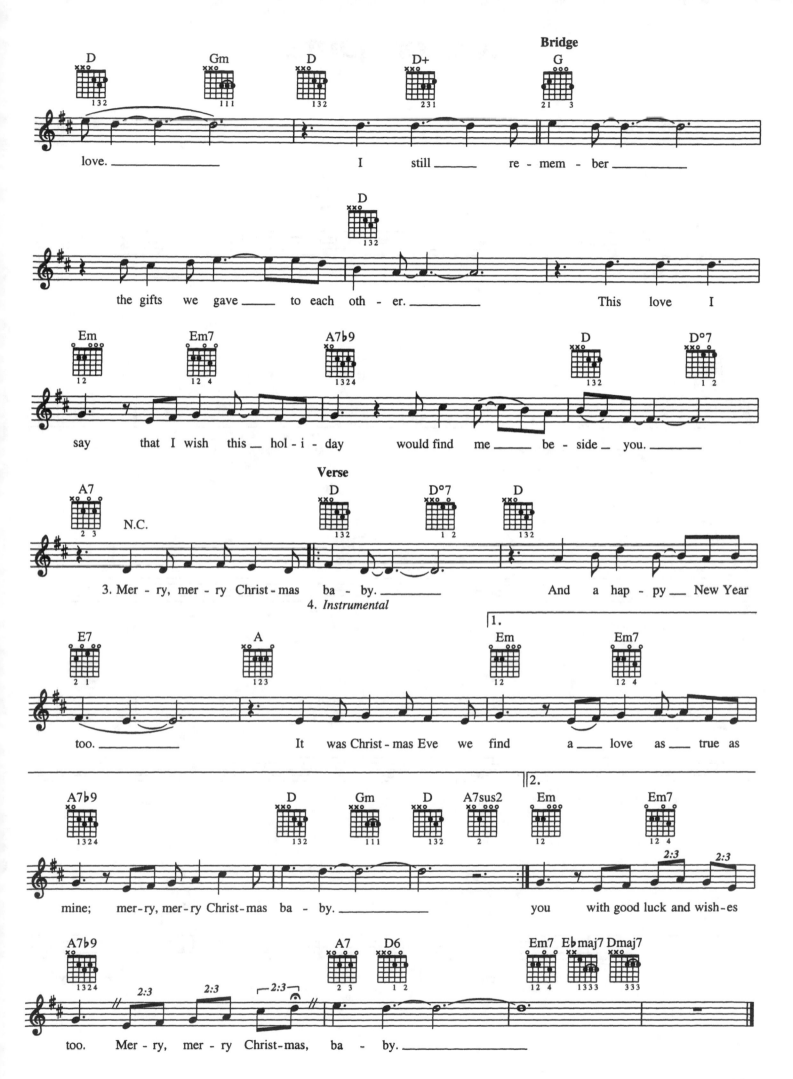

Mister Santa

Words and Music by Pat Ballard

Strum Pattern: 4
Pick Pattern: 3

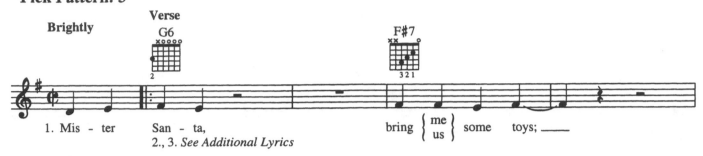

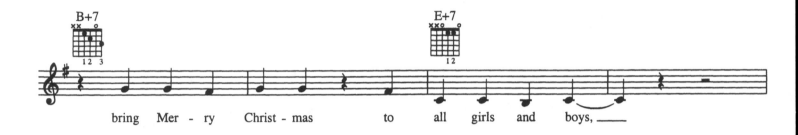

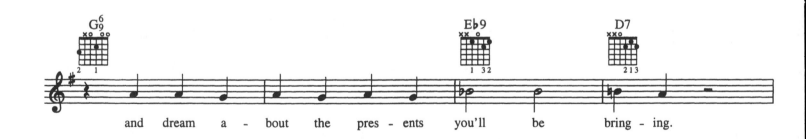

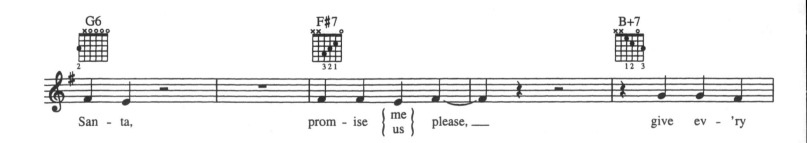

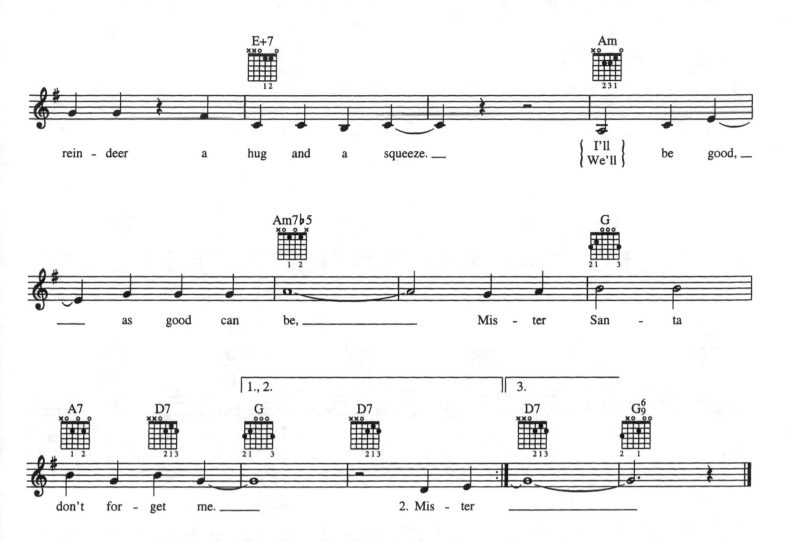

rein - deer a hug and a squeeze. ___ { I'll / We'll } be good, ___

___ as good can be, _____ Mis - ter San - ta

1., 2.

don't for - get me. _____

3.

2. Mis - ter _____

Additional Lyrics

2. Mister Santa, dear old Saint Nick
Be awful careful and please don't get sick.
Put on your coat when breezes are blowin'
And when you cross the street look where you're goin'.
Santa, we (I) love you so,
We (I) hope you never get lost in the snow.
Take your time when you unpack,
Mister Santa don't hurry back.

3. Mister Santa, we've been so good.
We've washed the dishes and done what we should.
Made up the beds and scrubbed up our toesies.
We've used a kleenex when we've blown our nosesies.
Santa look at our ears, they're clean as whistles.
We're sharper than shears.
Now we've put you on the spot,
Mister Santa bring us a lot.

The Most Wonderful Day of the Year

Music and Lyrics by Johnny Marks

Strum Pattern: 7
Pick Pattern: 7
Intro
Freely

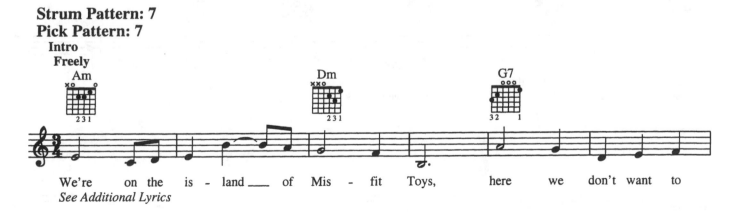

We're on the is - land ___ of Mis - fit Toys, here we don't want to
See Additional Lyrics

ga - lore _____ scat - tered on the floor. _____ There's no room for more _____ and it's all be - cause of San - ta Claus! A scoot - er for Jim - my, a dol - ly for Sue, the kind that will e - ven say "How do ya do!" When Christ - mas Day is here. _____ The most

1. *won - der - ful day of the year. _____*

2. *2. A won - der - ful, won - der - ful, won - der - ful, won - der - ful, won - der - ful day of _____ the year! _____*

Additional Lyrics

Intro Up at the North Pole they have their laws,
Elves must work ev'ry day.
Making the toys that Old Santa Claus
Leads upon his sleigh.

Chorus When Christmas Day is here,
The most wonderful day of the year!
Spirits gay; ev'ryone will say, "Happy Holiday!
And the best to you all the whole year through."
An electric train hidden high on a shelf
That Daddy gives David but then runs himself.
When Christmas Day is here,
The most wonderful, wonderful, wonderful,
Wonderful, wonderful day of the year!

Most of All I Wish You Were Here

Music and Lyrics by Denise Osso

*Strum Pattern: 4
*Pick Pattern: 3

*Use Pattern 7 for 3/4 meas. & Pattern 10 for 2/4 meas.

know ___ that most of all I wish you were here.

Verse

2. I've sent my cards and trimmed the tree,

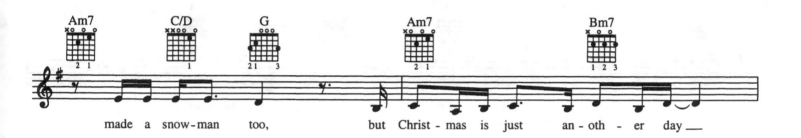

made a snow-man too, but Christ-mas is just an-oth-er day ___

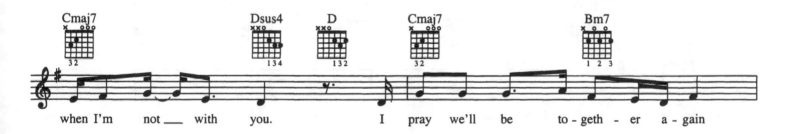

when I'm not ___ with you. I pray we'll be to-geth-er a-gain

just like we used to be, I send you my love. You can keep it 'til then,

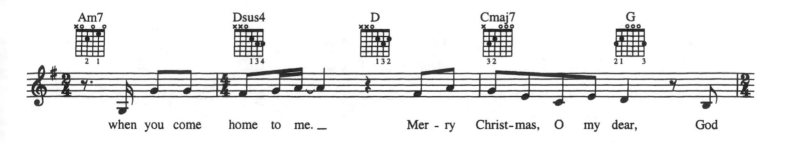

when you come home to me. ___ Mer-ry Christ-mas, O my dear, God

keep you safe from harm. When you come home I'll still be here to

Outro

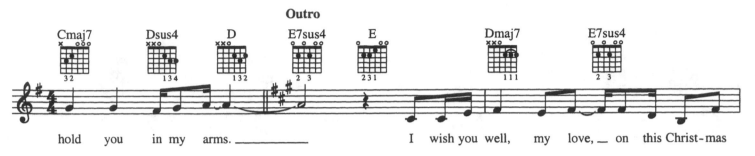

hold you in my arms. _____ I wish you well, my love, __ on this Christ-mas

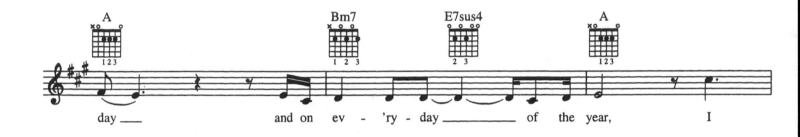

day __ and on ev - 'ry - day _____ of the year, I

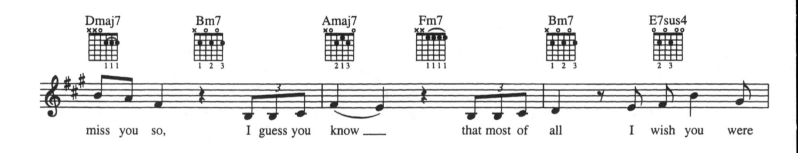

miss you so, I guess you know ___ that most of all I wish you were

Freely

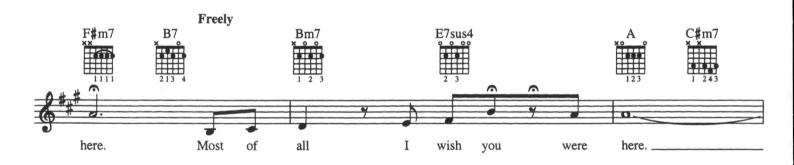

here. Most of all I wish you were here. _____

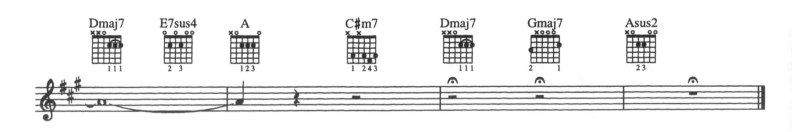

Must Be Santa

Words and Music by Hal Moore and Bill Fredricks

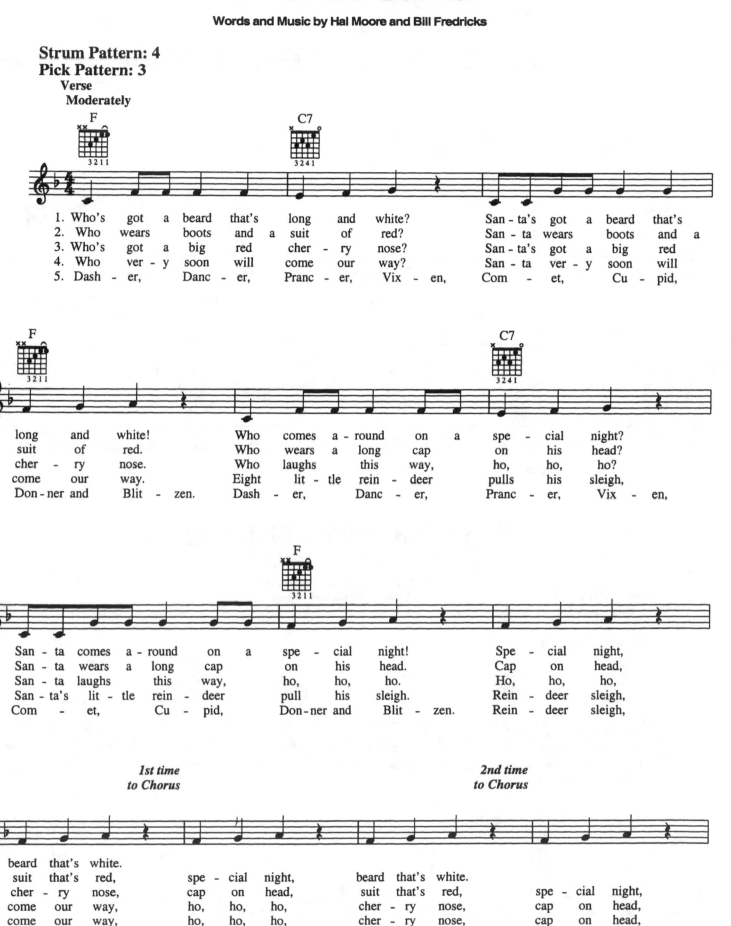

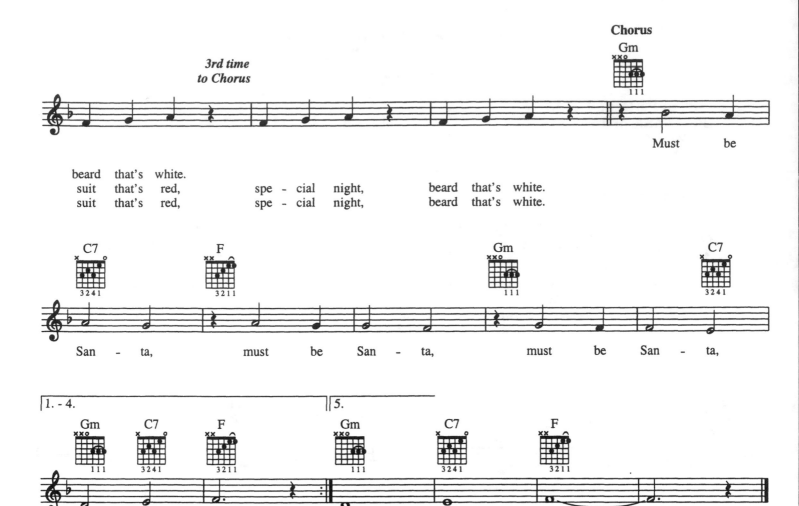

3rd time to Chorus

Chorus
Gm

Must be

beard that's white.
suit that's red, spe - cial night, beard that's white.
suit that's red, spe - cial night, beard that's white.

C7   F   Gm   C7

San - ta, must be San - ta, must be San - ta,

|1. - 4.
Gm   C7   F

|5.
Gm   C7   F

San - ta Claus. San - ta Claus. _____

My Favorite Things
from THE SOUND OF MUSIC

Lyrics by Oscar Hammerstein II
Music by Richard Rodgers

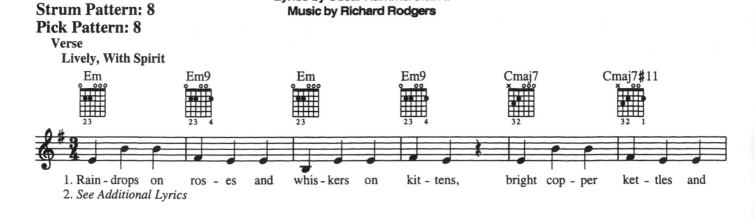

Strum Pattern: 8
Pick Pattern: 8
Verse
Lively, With Spirit

Em   Em9   Em   Em9   Cmaj7   Cmaj7#11

1. Rain - drops on ros - es and whis - kers on kit - tens, bright cop - per ket - tles and
2. *See Additional Lyrics*

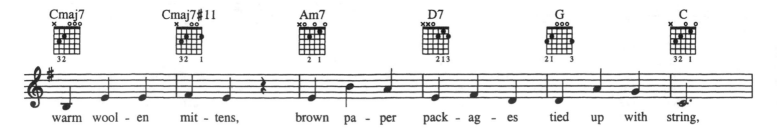

Cmaj7   Cmaj7#11   Am7   D7   G   C

warm wool - en mit - tens, brown pa - per pack - ag - es tied up with string,

these are a few of my fa - vor - ite things.

Verse

3. Girls in white dress - es with blue sat - in sash - es, snow - flakes that stay on my nose and eye - lash - es, sil - ver white win - ters that melt in - to springs, these are a few of my fa - vor - ite things.

Bridge

When the dog bites, when the bee stings, when I'm feel - ing sad, _____ I sim - ply re - mem - ber my fa - vor - ite things and then I don't feel so bad. _____

Additional Lyrics

2. Cream colored ponies and crisp apple strudles,
   Doorbells and sleigh bells and schnitzel with noodles,
   Wild geese that fly with the moon on their wings,
   These are a few of my favorite things.

159

The Most Wonderful Time of the Year

Words and Music by Eddie Pola and George Wyle

Strum Pattern: 7
Pick Pattern: 8

out in the snow. There'll be scar - y ghost stor - ies and

D.S. al Coda

tales of the glo - ries of Christ - mas - es long, long a - go. _____ 3. It's the

⊕ *Coda*

most won - der - ful time, it's the most won - der - ful

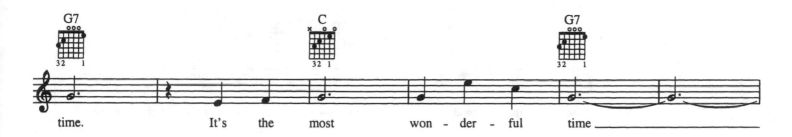

time. It's the most won - der - ful time _____

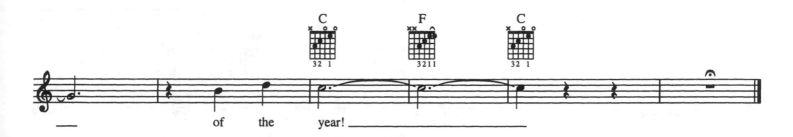

___ of the year! _____

Additional Lyrics

2. It's the hap-happiest season of all,
   With those holiday greetings
   And gay happy meetings
   When friends come to call.
   It's the hap-happiest season of all.

3. It's the most wonderful time of the year.
   There'll be much mistletoeing
   And hearts will be glowing
   When loved ones are near.
   It's the most wonderful time of the year.

Neighbor, What Has You So Excited?

Traditional French

Strum Pattern: 7
Pick Pattern: 7

Verse
Moderately

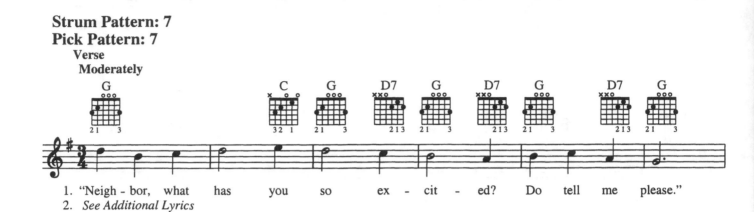

1. "Neigh - bor, what has you so ex - cit - ed? Do tell me please."
2. *See Additional Lyrics*

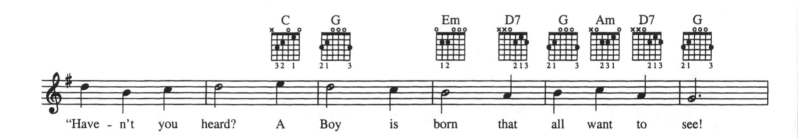

"Have - n't you heard? A Boy is born that all want to see!

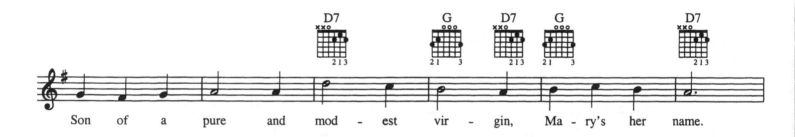

Son of a pure and mod - est vir - gin, Ma - ry's her name.

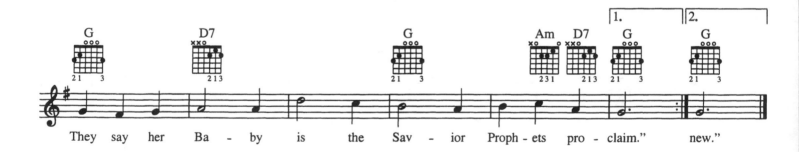

They say her Ba - by is the Sav - ior Proph - ets pro - claim." new."

Additional Lyrics

2. "It would be pleasant to go with you.
   Likely I'll go.
   But can't we take our time so see him?
   Why hurry so?
   Have you some cake to take the infant?
   Sugar-plums, too?
   I'm sure that Mary's house is lovely'
   Tidy and new."

The Night Before Christmas Song

Music by Johnny Marks
Lyrics adapted by Johnny Marks from Clement Moore's Poem

Strum Pattern: 8
Pick Pattern: 8

Verse
Brightly

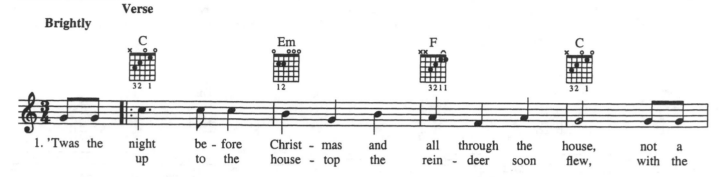

1. 'Twas the night be - fore Christ - mas and all through the house, not a
   up to the house - top the rein - deer soon flew, with the

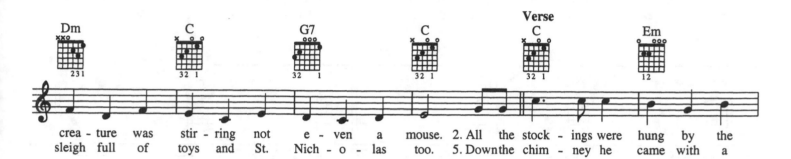

crea - ture was stir - ring not e - ven a mouse. 2. All the stock - ings were hung by the
sleigh full of toys and St. Nich - o - las too. 5. Down the chim - ney he came with a

chim - ney with care, in the hope that St. Nich - o - las soon would be there. Then
leap and a bound. He was dressed all in fur and his bel - ly was round. He

Bridge

what to my won - der - ing eyes should ap - pear, a min - ia - ture sleigh and eight
spoke not a word but went straight to his work and filled all the stock - ings; then

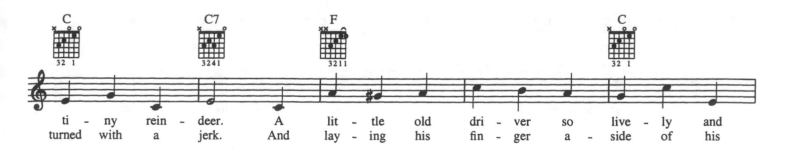

ti - ny rein - deer. A lit - tle old dri - ver so live - ly and
turned with a jerk. And lay - ing his fin - ger a - side of his

quick,   I   knew   in   a   mo - ment   it   must   be   St.   Nick.   3. And more

nose,   then   giv - ing   a   nod   up   the   chim - ney   he   rose;   6. But   I

Verse

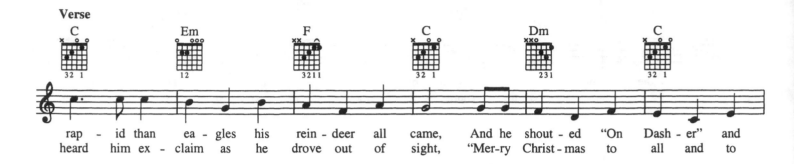

rap - id   than   ea - gles   his   rein - deer   all   came,   And   he   shout - ed   "On   Dash - er"   and

heard   him   ex - claim   as   he   drove   out   of   sight,   "Mer - ry   Christ - mas   to   all   and   to

1.

each   rein - deer's   name.   2.   4. And   so   all   a   good   night!"

Nuttin' for Christmas

Words and Music by Roy Bennett and Sid Tepper

Strum Pattern: 4
Pick Pattern: 5

Verse
Brightly

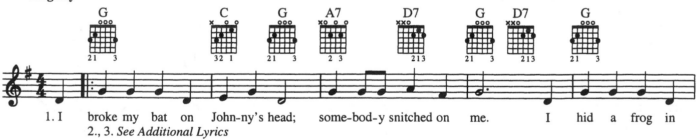

1. I   broke   my   bat   on   John - ny's   head;   some - bod - y   snitched   on   me.   I   hid   a   frog   in
2., 3. *See Additional Lyrics*

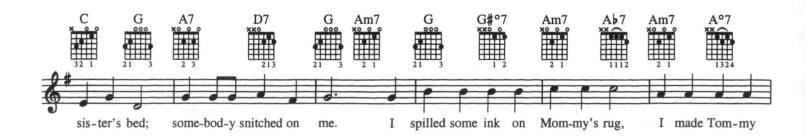

sis - ter's   bed;   some - bod - y   snitched   on   me.   I   spilled   some   ink   on   Mom - my's   rug,   I   made   Tom - my

eat a bug, bought some gum with a pen - ny slug; some - bod - y snitched on me. Oh,

Chorus

I'm get - tin' nut - tin' for Christ-mas. Mom - my and Dad - dy are

mad. I'm get - tin' nut - tin' for Christ-mas, 'cause

1., 2.

3.

I ain't been nut - tin' but bad._____ 2., 3. I bad._____ So you

Outro

bet - ter be good, what ev - er you do, 'cause if you're bad I'm warn - ing you,

You'll get nut - tin' for Christ - mas._____

Additional Lyrics

2. I put a tack on teacher's chair;
Somebody snitched on me.
I tied a knot in Susie's hair;
Somebody snitched on me.
I did a dance on Mommy's plants,
Climbed a tree and tore my pants.
Filled the sugar bowl with ants;
Somebody snitched on me.

3. I won't be seeing Santa Claus;
Somebody snitched on me.
He won't come visit me because
Somebody snitched on me.
Next year, I'll be going straight.
Next year, I'll be good, just wait.
I'd start now but it's too late;
Somebody snitched on me, Oh,

Noel! Noel!

French-English Carol

Strum Pattern: 4
Pick Pattern: 3

Verse
Rubato

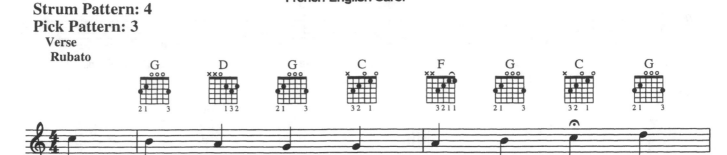

No - el! No - el! Good news I tell, and

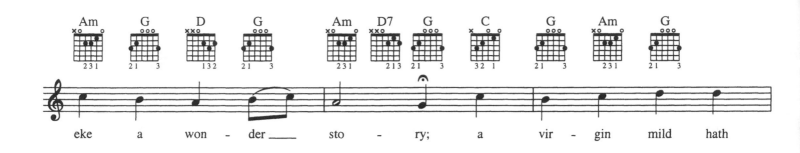

eke a won - der ___ sto - ry; a vir - gin mild hath

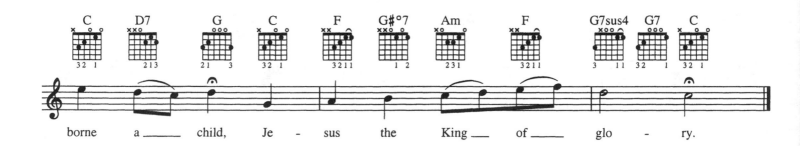

borne a ___ child, Je - sus the King ___ of ___ glo - ry.

Copyright © 2000 by HAL LEONARD CORPORATION

Rockin' Around the Christmas Tree

Music and Lyrics by Johnny Marks

Strum Pattern: 2, 6
Pick Pattern: 4, 6

Verse
Moderate Rock

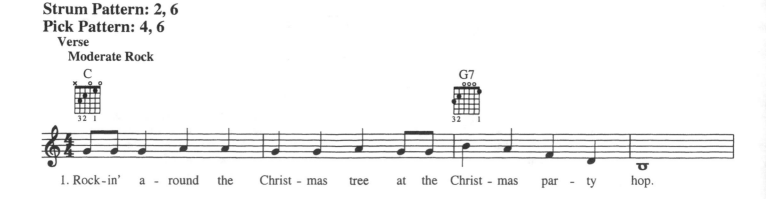

1. Rock-in' a - round the Christ - mas tree at the Christ - mas par - ty hop.

Mis - tle - toe hung where you can see ev - 'ry cou - ple tries to stop.

Rock - in' a - round the Christ - mas tree, let the Christ - mas spir - it ring.

La - ter we'll have some pump - kin pie and we'll do some car - ol - ing.

Bridge

You will get a sen - ti - men - tal feel - ing when you hear

voic - es sing - ing, "Let's be jol - ly. Deck the halls with boughs of hol - ly."

Verse

2. Rock - in' a - round the Christ - mas tree, have a hap - py hol - i - day. Ev - 'ry - one danc - ing

mer - ri - ly in the new old fash - ioned way. new old fash - ioned way. _____

O Bethlehem

Traditional Spanish

Verse
Slowly

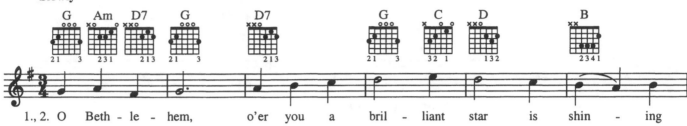

1., 2. O Beth - le - hem, o'er you a bril - liant star is shin - ing

Outro

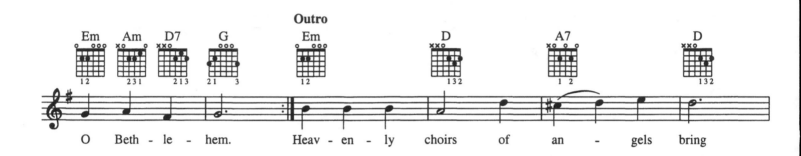

O Beth - le - hem. Heav - en - ly choirs of an - gels bring

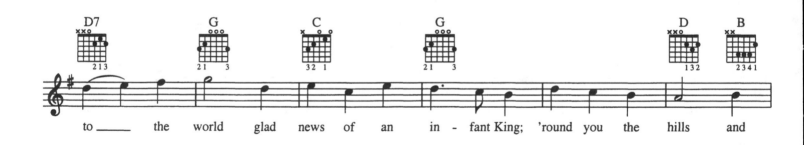

to _____ the world glad news of an in - fant King; 'round you the hills and

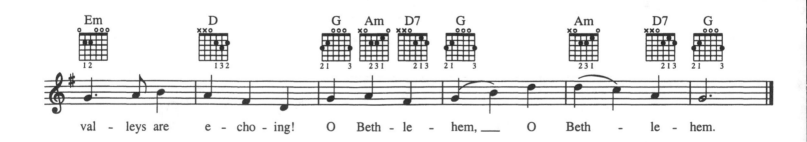

val - leys are e - cho - ing! O Beth - le - hem, ___ O Beth - le - hem.

O Christmas Tree

Traditional German Carol

Strum Pattern: 8, 7
Pick Pattern: 8, 9
Verse
Moderately

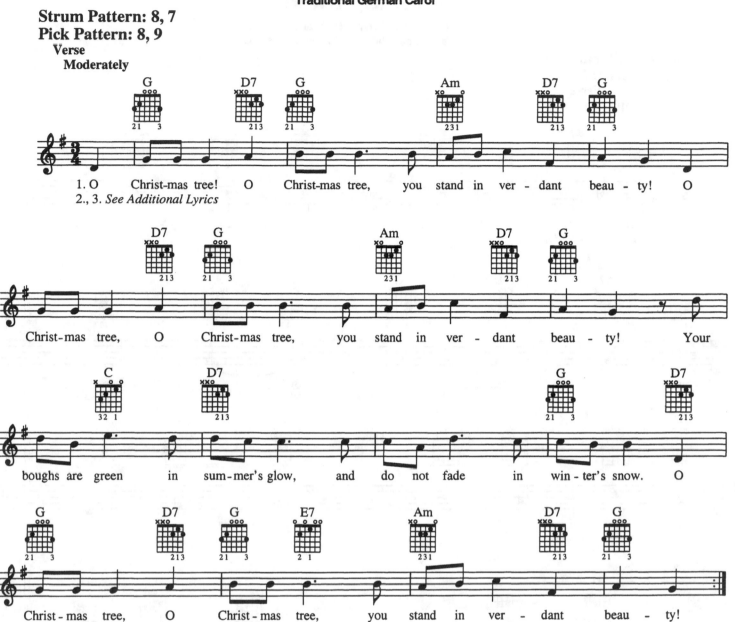

1. O Christmas tree! O Christmas tree, you stand in verdant beauty! O
2., 3. *See Additional Lyrics*

Christmas tree, O Christmas tree, you stand in verdant beauty! Your

boughs are green in summer's glow, and do not fade in winter's snow. O

Christmas tree, O Christmas tree, you stand in verdant beauty!

Additional Lyrics

2. O, Christmas tree! O, Christmas tree,
   Much pleasure doth thou bring me!
   O, Christmas tree! O, Christmas tree,
   Much pleasure does thou bring me!
   For every year the Christmas tree
   Brings to us all both joy and glee.
   O, Christmas tree, O, Christmas tree,
   Much pleasure doth thou bring me!

3. O, Christmas tree! O, Christmas tree,
   Thy candles shine out brightly!
   O, Christmas Tree, O, Christmas tree,
   Thy candles shine out brightly!
   Each bough doth hold its tiny light
   That makes each toy to sparkle bright.
   O, Christmas tree, O Christmas tree,
   Thy candles shine out brightly.

O Come, All Ye Faithful
(Adeste Fideles)

Words and Music by John Francis Wade
Latin Words translated by Frederick Oakeley

Strum Pattern: 4
Pick Pattern: 5
Verse
Triumphantly

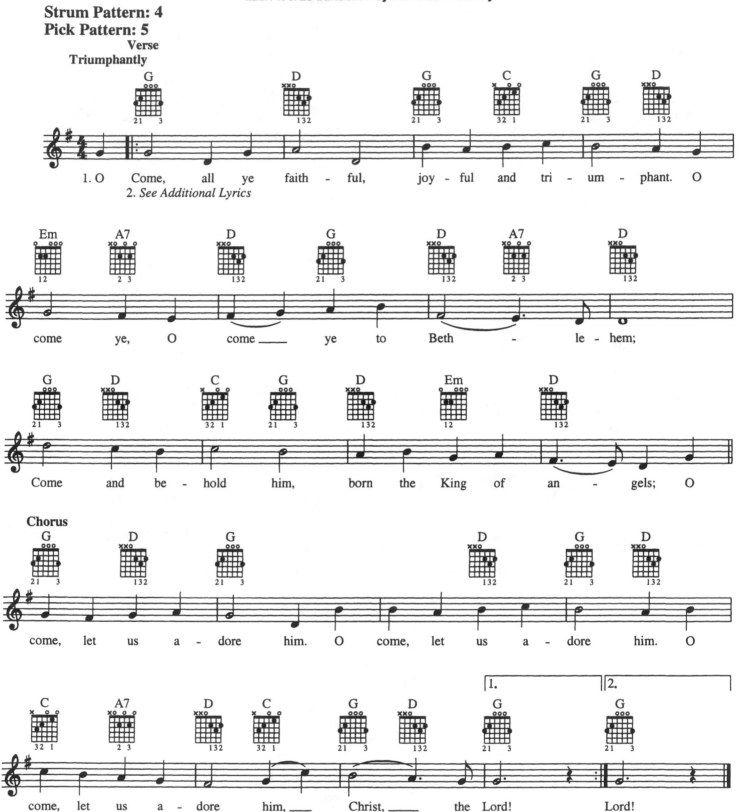

Additional Lyrics

2. Sing choirs of angels, sing in exultation.
   O sing all ye citizens of heaven above.
   Glory to God in the highest.

O Come, O Come Immanuel

Plainsong, 13th Century
Words translated by John M. Neale and Henry S. Coffin

Strum Pattern: 4
Pick Pattern: 5

Verse
Slowly And Expressively

1. O come, O come Im - man - u - el, and
2. *See Additional Lyrics*

ran - som cap - tive Is - ra - el, that mourns in lone - ly

ex - ile here un - til the Son of God _____ ap -

Chorus

pear. Re - joice, re - joice! Im - man - u -

el shall come to thee, O Is - ra - el!

Additional Lyrics

2. O come, Thou Key Of David, come
   And open wide our heav'nly home.
   Make safe the way that leads on high
   And close the path to misery.

O Come, Little Children

Words by C. von Schmidt
Music by J.P.A. Schulz

Strum Pattern: 10
Pick Pattern: 10

Verse
Quietly

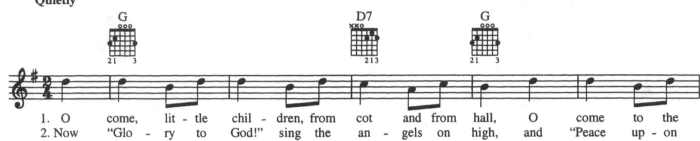

1. O come, lit - tle chil - dren, from cot and from hall, O come to the
2. Now "Glo - ry to God!" sing the an - gels on high, and "Peace up - on

man - ger in Beth - le - hem's stall. There meek - ly He li - eth, the
earth!" heav'n - ly voic - es re - ply. Then come lit - tle chil - dren and

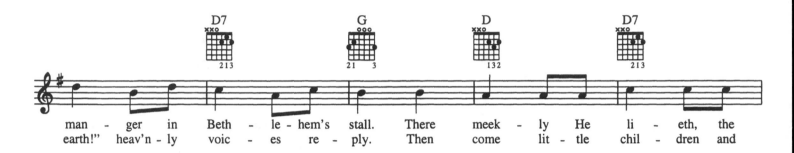

heav - en - ly child, so poor and so hum - ble, so sweet and so mild.
join in the day that glad - dened the world on that first Christ - mas day.

Pretty Paper

Words and Music by Willie Nelson

Strum Pattern: 8, 7
Pick Pattern: 8, 9

Verse
Slowly, With Expression

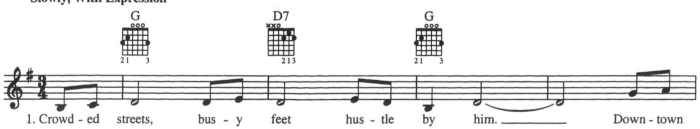

1. Crowd - ed streets, bus - y feet hus - tle by him. _____ Down - town

O Day

New Words and New Music Adaption by Bessie Jones and St. Simon Island Singers
Edited with New Material by Alan Lomax

Strum Pattern: 4
Pick Pattern: 3

Verse
Moderately

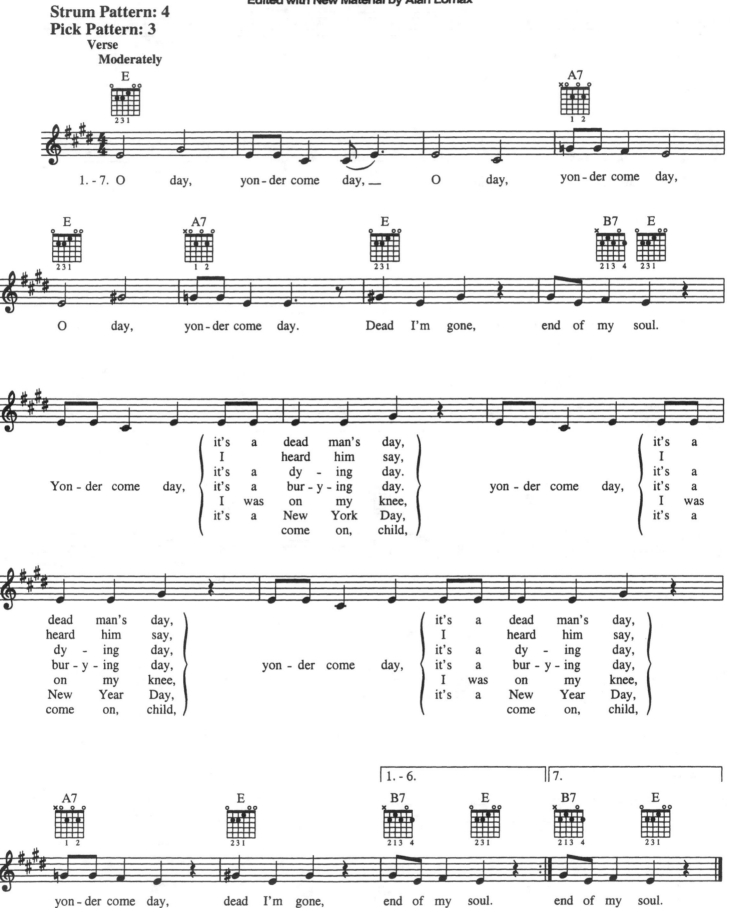

O Hearken Ye

Lyric by Wihla Hutson
Music by Alfred Burt

Strum Pattern: 4
Pick Pattern: 3

1. O heark - en ye who would be-lieve, the gra-cious ti - dings now re-ceive:
2., 3. *See Additional Lyrics*

Glo - ri - a, glo - ri - a, in ex - cel - sis De - o. The

might - y Lord of heav'n and earth, to - day is come to hu - man birth.

Glo - ri - a, glo - ri - a, in ex - cel - sis De - o. 2. O De - o.

Additional Lyrics

2. O hearken, ye who long for peace,
   Your troubled searching now may cease.
   Gloria, gloria, in excelsis Deo.
   For at his cradle you shall find
   God's healing grace for all mankind.
   Gloria, gloria, in excelsis Deo.

3. O hearken, ye who long for love,
   And turn your hearts to God above.
   Gloria, gloria, in excelsis Deo.
   The angel's song the wonder tells:
   New Love Incarnate with us dwells.
   Gloria, gloria, in excelsis Deo.

O Holy Night

French Words by Placide Cappeau
English Words by John S. Dwight
Music by Adolphe Adam

Strum Pattern: 7, 9
Pick Pattern: 7, 9

Verse
Slow And Flowing

1. O Holy night ____ the stars are bright - ly shin - ing, it is the
2. Tru - ly He taught us to love ____ one an - oth - er. His law is

night of the dear Sav - ior's birth. _____ Long lay the world ____ in
love, and His gos - pel is peace. _____ Chains shall He break, for the

sin and er - ror pin - ing, 'til He ap - peared and the soul felt its
slave ____ is our broth - er, and in His name all op - pres - sion shall

worth. _____ A thrill of hope the wear - y soul re -
cease. _____ Sweet hymns of joy in grate - ful cho - rus

joic - es, for yon - der breaks a new and glor - ious morn.
raise we. Let all with - in us praise His ho - ly name.

O Little Town of Bethlehem

Words by Phillips Brooks
Music by Lewis H. Redner

Strum Pattern: 4
Pick Pattern: 5

Verse
Quietly

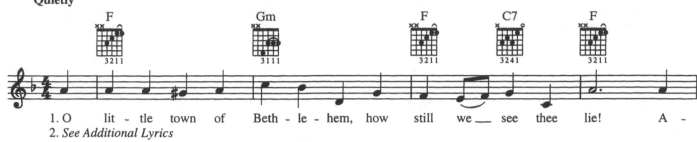

1. O lit - tle town of Beth - le - hem, how still we __ see thee lie! A -
2. *See Additional Lyrics*

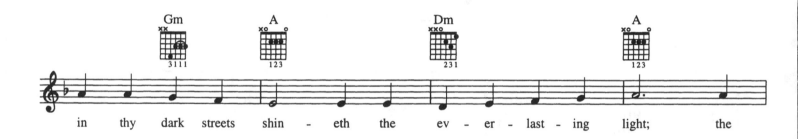

bove thy deep and dream - less sleep, the si - lent __ stars go by; yet

in thy dark streets shin - eth the ev - er - last - ing light; the

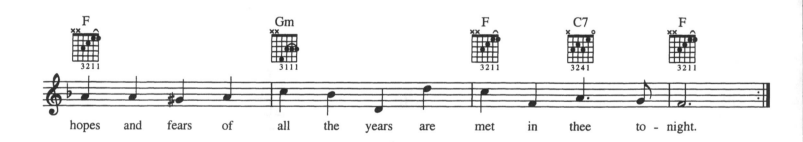

hopes and fears of all the years are met in thee to - night.

Additional Lyrics

2. For Christ is born of Mary, and gathered all above.
   While mortals sleep the angels keep
   Their watch of wond'ring love.
   O morning stars, together proclaim the holy birth!
   And praises sing to God the King,
   And peace to men on earth!

O Sanctissima

Sicilian Carol

Strum Pattern: 4
Pick Pattern: 3

Verse
Joyfully

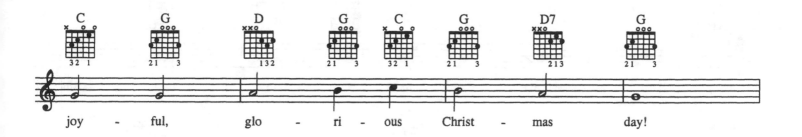

Day of ho - li - ness, ___ peace and hap - pi - ness, ___

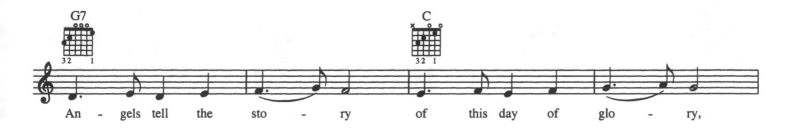

joy - ful, glo - ri - ous Christ - mas day!

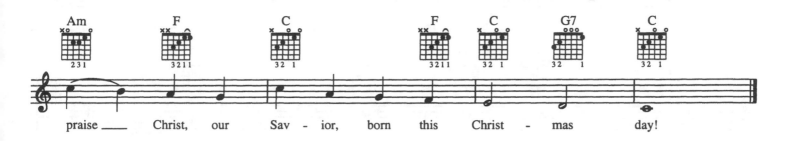

An - gels tell the sto - ry of this day of glo - ry,

praise ___ Christ, our Sav - ior, born this Christ - mas day!

An Old Fashioned Christmas

Music and Lyrics by Johnny Marks

Strum Pattern: 4
Pick Pattern: 1, 3

Verse
Moderately

Old Toy Trains

Words and Music by Roger Miller

Strum Pattern: 3
Pick Pattern: 3

man dressed in white and red. Lit-tle boy ___ don't ___ you think it's time you were in

1. bed? So close your bed?

2. Lit-tle boy ___ don't ___ you think it's time you were in bed?

One Bright Star

Words and Music by John Jarvis

Strum Pattern: 4
Pick Pattern: 3

Intro
Moderately Slow

Long, long, ___ a - go in a world dark ___ and cold, _____ a night so

still, win-ter's chill, one bright star ___ was shin - ing. 1. On a

Verse

bed made ___ of hay in a man - ger ___ He lay. _____ The shep-herds

this Christ - mas day may that star light ___ your way. _____ This Christ-mas

On Christmas Night
(Sussex Carol)
Sussex Carol

Strum Pattern: 8
Pick Pattern: 8

Verse
Moderately Slow

1. On Christ - mas Night, true Christ - ians sings, to hear the news __ the
2., 3., 4. *See Additional Lyrics*

an - gels bring. Christ - mas Night, true Christ - ians sings, to hear the news __ the

an - gels bring. News of great joy __ and of __ great mirth,

1., 2., 3. | 4.

ti - dings of our dear Sav - ior's birth. _____

Additional Lyrics

2. The King of Kings to us is giv'n,
The Lord of earth and King of heav'n;
The King of Kings to us is giv'n,
The Lord of earth and King of Heav'n;
Angels and men with joy may sing
Of blest Jesus, their newborn King.

3. So how on earth can men be sad,
When Jesus comes to make us glad?
So how on earth can man be sad,
When Jesus comes to make us glad?
From all our sins to set us free,
Buying for us our liberty.

4. From out the darkness have we light,
Which makes the angels sing this night.
From out the darkness have we light,
Which makes the angels sing this night.
"Glory to God, His peace to men,
And good will, evermore! Amen."

Once in Royal David's City

Words by Cecil F. Alexander
Music by Henry J. Gauntlett

Strum Pattern: 4
Pick Pattern: 5

Verse
Quietly

1. Once in roy - al Da - vid's cit - y, stood a low - ly cat - tle __ shed,

where a moth - er laid __ her __ ba - by in a man - ger for __ His __ bed.

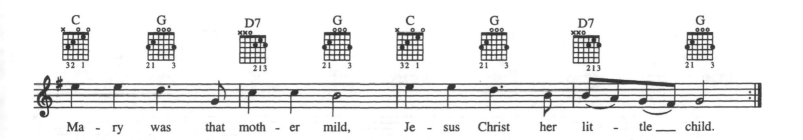

Ma - ry was that moth - er mild, Je - sus Christ her lit - tle __ child.

Additional Lyrics

2. And our eyes at last shall see Him,
Through His own redeeming love.
For that child so dear and gentle
Is our Lord in heav'n above.
And He leads His children on
To the place where He is gone.

One for the Little Bitty Baby
(Go Where I Send Thee)

Spiritual Arranged by Ronnie Gilbert, Lee Hays, Fred Hellerman and Pete Seeger

Strum Pattern: 4
Pick Pattern: 3

1. Chil - dren, (2. - 10.) go where I send thee! How shall I send thee?

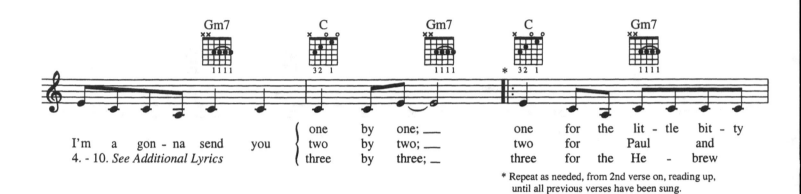

I'm a gon - na send you
4. - 10. *See Additional Lyrics*

{ one by one; ___ one for the lit - tle bit - ty
{ two by two; ___ two for Paul and
{ three by three; ___ three for the He - brew

* Repeat as needed, from 2nd verse on, reading up,
until all previous verses have been sung.

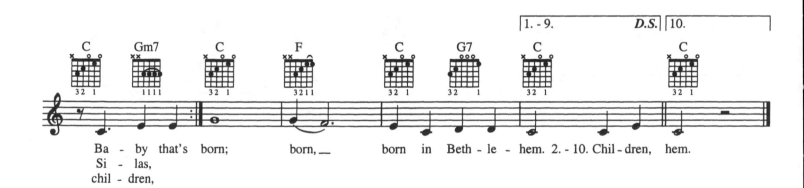

Ba - by that's born; born, ___ born in Beth - le - hem. 2. - 10. Chil - dren, hem.
Si - las,
chil - dren,

Additional Lyrics

4. I'm a-gonna send you four by four;
   four for the four that stood by the door,

5. I'm a-gonna send you five by five;
   five for the gospel preachers,

6. I'm a-gonna send you six by six;
   six for the six that never got fixed,

7. I'm a-gonna send you seven by seven;
   seven for the seven that never got to heaven,

8. I'm a-gonna send you eight by eight;
   eight for the eight that stood at the gate,

9. I'm a-gonna send you nine by nine;
   nine for the nine all dressed so fine,

10. I'm a-gonna send you ten by ten;
    ten for the ten commandments,

Pat-A-Pan
(Willie, Take Your Little Drum)

Words and Music by Bernard de la Monnoye

Strum Pattern: 2, 3
Pick Pattern: 2, 3

Verse
Very Fast

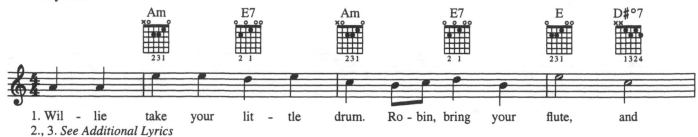

1. Wil - lie take your lit - tle drum. Ro - bin, bring your flute, and
2., 3. *See Additional Lyrics*

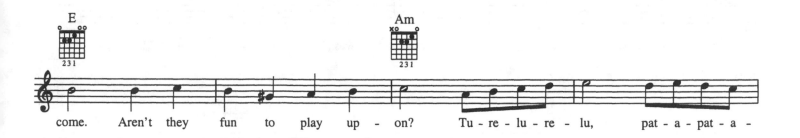

come. Aren't they fun to play up - on? Tu - re - lu - re - lu, pat - a - pat - a -

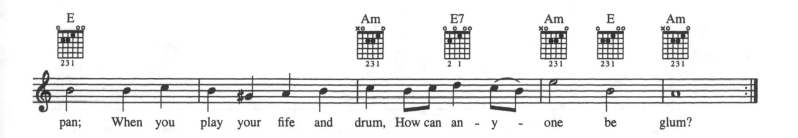

pan; When you play your fife and drum, How can an - y - one be glum?

Additional Lyrics

2. When the men of olden days
   Gave the King of Kings their praise,
   They had pipes to play upon.
   Tu-re-lu-re-lu, pat-a-pat-a-pan.
   And also the drums they'd play.
   Full of joy, on Christmas Day.

3. God and man today become
   Closely joined as flute and drum.
   Let the joyous tune play on!
   Tu-re-lu-re-lu, pat-a-pat-a-pan.
   As the instruments you play,
   We will sing, this Christmas Day.

Out of the East

Words and Music by Harry Noble

Strum Pattern: 7
Pick Pattern: 7

Verse

1. Out of the East there came rid - ing, rid - ing, three of the
2., 3. *See Additional Lyrics*

wis - est of men, _____ dust was their en - e - my blind - ing,

blind - ing, e - ven the wis - est of them. _____

Bridge

1. Wan - der - ing shep - herds heard tell their sto - ry, told in the
2., 3. *See Additional Lyrics*

flick - er - ing fire - light, ten - der light, ev - er bright Christ - mas night.

Outro

1. Far to the West was there shin - ing, shin - ing, blaz - ing a
2., 3. *See Additional Lyrics*

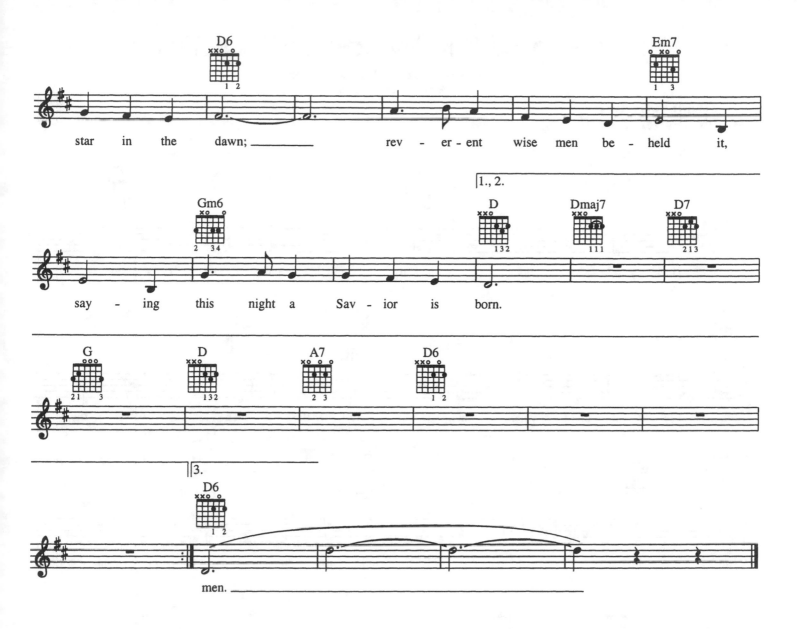

star   in   the   dawn; _____   rev - er - ent   wise   men   be - held   it,

say - ing   this   night   a   Sav - ior   is   born.

men. _____

Additional Lyrics

2. Into the West they went riding,
   Riding, following after the star,
   Over a quiet town shining, shining,
   Lighting their way from afar.

Bridge 2. Under its glory sat mother Mary,
   Tenderly singing a lullabye,
   Hushabye, don't you cry, lullabye.

Outro 2. Into the stable came riding, riding,
   Three of the wisest of men;
   Gifts did they bring for that babe in manger;
   Gifts for the Savior of men.

3. Low in a manger they found Him,
   Found Him, bathed in the light of yon star,
   Gold did they bring Him and frank-incense
   And myrhh from a land that was far.

Bridge 3. Shepherds crept in singing praises, praises,
   Angels kept watch to be near to Him,
   Dear to Him, One with Him, praising Him.

Outro 3. Into the east then went riding, riding,
   Three of the wisest of men;
   Found was the Babe in a lowly manger,
   Crowned was the Savior of men.

Parade of the Wooden Soldiers

English Lyrics by Ballard MacDonald
Music by Leon Jessel

Strum Pattern: 2
Pick Pattern: 3

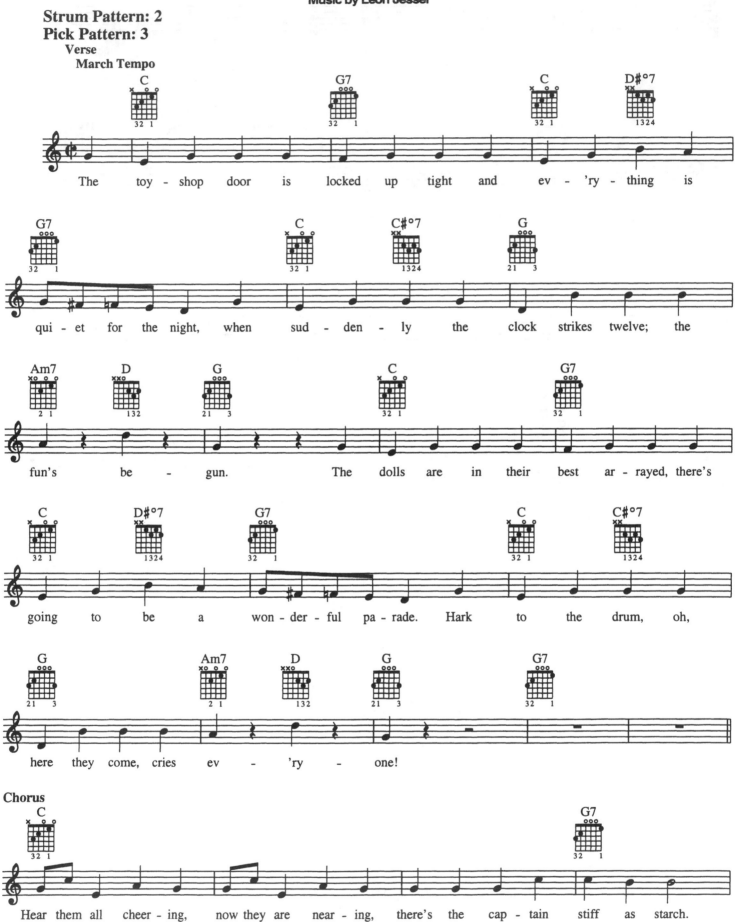

Please Come Home for Christmas

Words and Music by Charles Brown and Gene Redd

Strum Pattern: 8
Pick Pattern: 8

Additional Lyrics

2. Choirs will be singing "Silent Night,"
   Christmas carols by candlelight.
   Please come home for Christmas,
   Please come home for Christmas;
   If not for Christmas, by New Year's night.

Poor Little Jesus

Arranged by Ronnie Gilbert, Lee Hays, Fred Hellerman and Pete Seeger

Strum Pattern: 3
Pick Pattern: 4

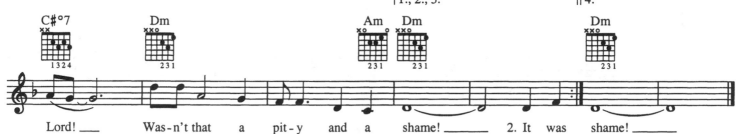

Additional Lyrics

2. It was Poor Little Jesus, yes, yes;
   Child of Mary, yes, yes;
   Didn't have no shelter, yes, yes;
   Wasn't that a pity and a shame, oh Lord!
   Wasn't that a pity and a shame!

3. It was Poor Little Jesus, yes, yes;
   They whipped Him up a mountain, yes, yes;
   And they hung Him with a robber, yes, yes;
   Wasn't that a pity and a shame, oh Lord!
   Wasn't that a pity and a shame!

4. He was born on Christmas, yes, yes;
   He was born on Christmas, yes, yes;
   Didn't have no cradle, yes, yes;
   Wasn't that a pity and a shame, oh Lord!
   Wasn't that a pity and a shame!

Ring Out, Ye Wild and Merry Bells

Words and Music by C. Maitland

Strum Pattern: 8
Pick Pattern: 8

Additional Lyrics

2. Ring out, ye silv'ry bells, ring out.
   Bring out your exultation
   That God with man is reconciled.
   Go tell it to the nations!
   Therefore let us all today,
   Glory in the highest!
   Banish sorrow far away,
   Glory in the highest!

Rejoice and Be Merry

Gallery Carol

Strum Pattern: 7
Pick Pattern: 7

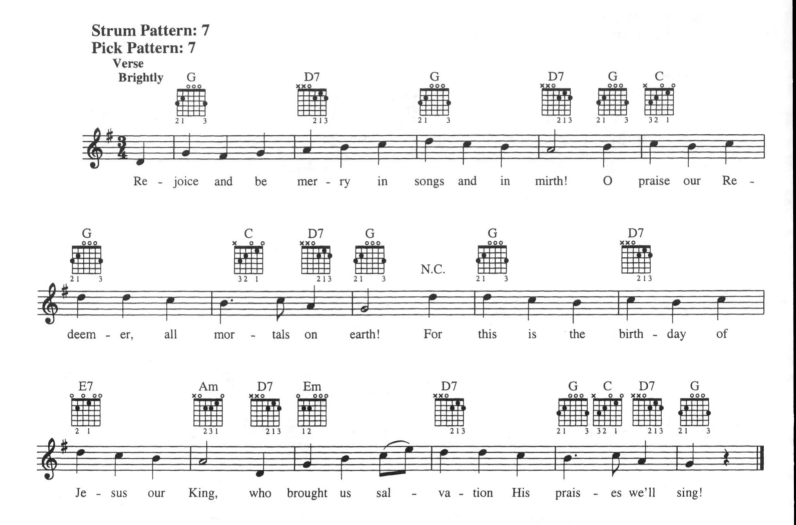

Re - joice and be mer - ry in songs and in mirth! O praise our Re -

deem - er, all mor - tals on earth! For this is the birth - day of

Je - sus our King, who brought us sal - va - tion His prais - es we'll sing!

R2D2, We Wish You a Merry Christmas

Words and Music by Don Oriolo and Meco Monardo

Strum Pattern: 4
Pick Pattern: 3

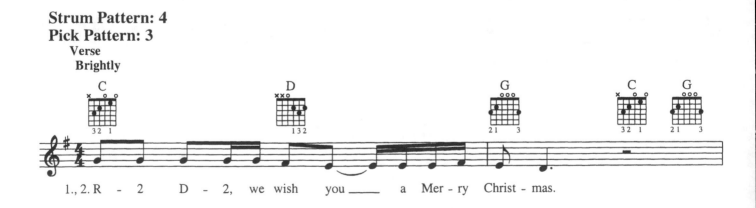

1., 2. R - 2 D - 2, we wish you ___ a Mer - ry Christ - mas.

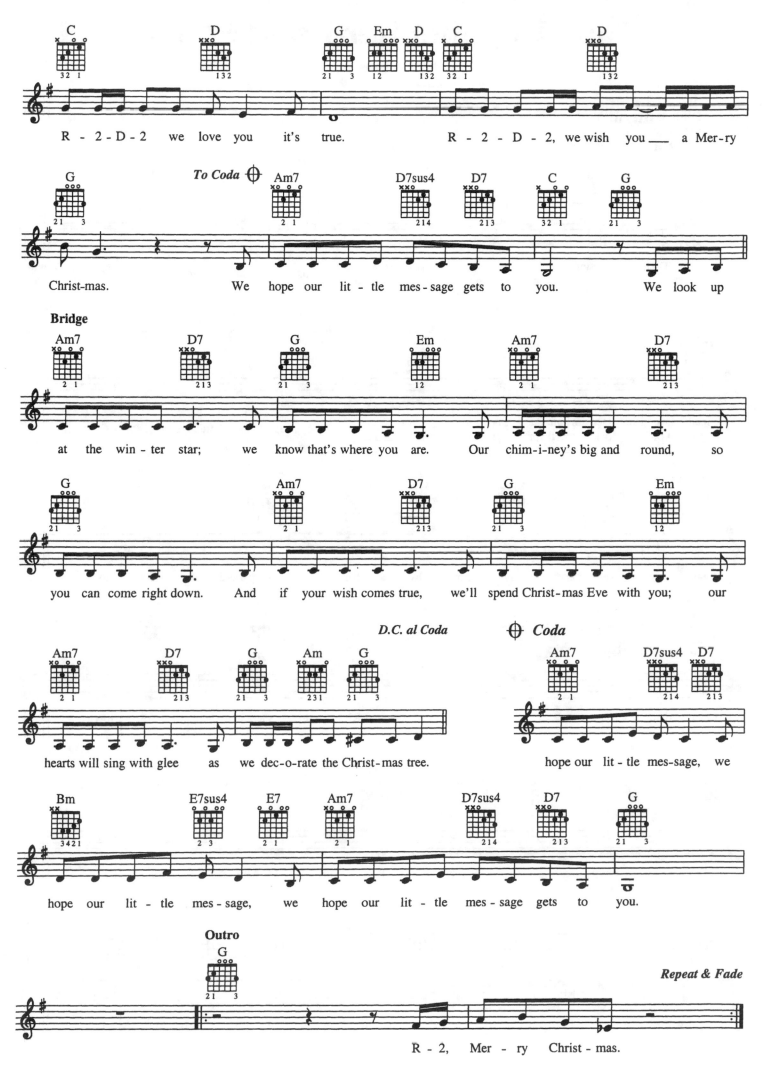

Rise Up, Shepherd, and Follow

African-American Spiritual

Strum Pattern: 3
Pick Pattern: 3
Verse
Fast

1. There's a star in the east on Christ-mas morn.
take good heed to the an-gel's word. } Rise up, shepherd and fol-low. { It will
You'll for-

lead to the place where the sav-ior's born. ___
get your flock, you'll for-get your herd. ___ } Rise up, shep-herd and fol-low.

Leave your ewes and leave your lambs. Rise up shep-herd and fol-low.

Leave your sheep and leave your rams. Rise up shep-herd and fol-low.

Chorus

Fol - low, fol - low. Rise up shep-herd and fol-low.

Fol-low the star of Beth-le-hem. ___ Rise up shep-herd and fol-low. 2. If you fol-low.

Santa, Bring My Baby Back (To Me)

Words and Music by Claude DeMetruis and Aaron Schroeder

Strum Pattern: 4
Pick Pattern: 3

Outro

fill my socks with can - dy, no bright and shin - y toy. You

wan - na make me hap - py and fill my heart with joy. Then, San - ta, hear my

plea. ___ San - ta, bring my ba - by back to me. ___

Additional Lyrics

2. The Christmas tree is ready.
   The candles all aglow.
   But with my baby far away
   What good is mistletoe?
   Oh, Santa, hear my plea.
   Santa, bring my baby back to me.

Shake Me I Rattle
(Squeeze Me I Cry)

Words and Music by Hal Hackady and Charles Naylor

Strum Pattern: 4
Pick Pattern: 7

Intro
Moderately

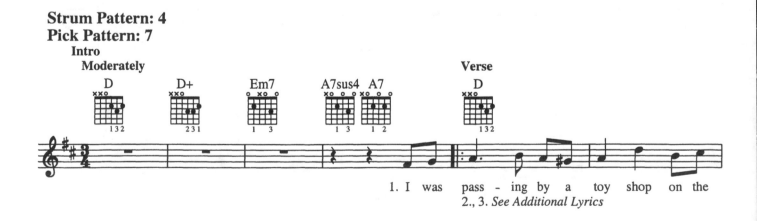

1. I was pass - ing by a toy shop on the
2., 3. *See Additional Lyrics*

Additional Lyrics

2. I recalled another toy shop on a square so long ago
Where I saw a little dolly that I wanted so
I remembered, I remembered how I longed to make it mine.
And around that other dolly hung another little sign:

3. It was late and snow was falling as the shoppers hurried by,
Past the girlie at the window with her little head held high.
They were closing up the toy shop as I hurried through the door.
Just in time to buy the dolly that her heart was longing for.

Rudolph the Red-Nosed Reindeer

Music and Lyrics by Johnny Marks

Intro
Freely

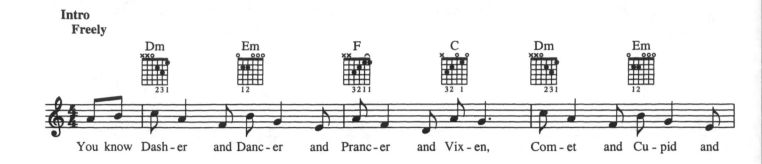

You know Dash-er and Danc-er and Pranc-er and Vix-en, Com-et and Cu-pid and

Don-ner and Blitz-en, but do you re-call the most fa-mous rein-deer of all.

Strum Pattern: 2, 3
Pick Pattern: 2, 3

Verse
Lightly

Ru-dolph, the red-nosed rein-deer had a ver-y shin-y nose,

and if you ev-er saw it, you would e-ven say it glows.

All of the oth-er rein-deer used to laugh and call him names,

they nev - er let poor Ru - dolph join in an - y rein - deer games.

Bridge

Then one fog - gy Christ - mas Eve, San - ta came to say,

"Ru - dolph, with your nose so bright, won't you guide my sleigh to - night?" —

Verse

Then how the rein - deer loved him as they shout - ed out with glee;

1.

"Ru - dolph, the red - nosed rein - deer, you'll go down in his - to - ry!"

2.

you'll go down in his - to - ry!" _____

Santa Baby

By Joan Javits, Phil Springer and Tony Springer

Strum Pattern: 1, 3
Pick Pattern: 2, 3

Intro
Moderately Slow

Mis - ter "Claus," I feel as though I know ya, _____ so you won't mind if I should get fam -

mil - ya, will ya?

1. San - ta ba - by, just slip a sa - ble un - der the tree _
4. *See Additional Lyrics*

_____ for me; ___ been an aw - ful good girl. ___ San - ta ba - by, so

hur - ry down the chim - ney to - night. _____

2. San - ta ba - by, a
5. *See Additional Lyrics*

fif - ty four con - vert - i - ble, too, ___ light blue. ___ I'll wait up for you dear. _

Additional Lyrics

4. Santa baby, one little thing I really do need;
   The deed to a platinum mine.
   Santa honey, so hurry down the chimney tonight.

5. Santa cutie and fill my stocking with a duplex and cheques.
   Sign your X on the line.
   Santa cutie, and hurry down the chimney tonight.

Bridge Come and trim my Christmas tree
   With some decorations at Tiffany.
   I really do believe in you.
   Let's see if you believe in me.

6. Santa baby, forgot to mention one little thing, a ring!
   I don't mean on the phone.
   Santa baby, so hurry down the chimney tonight.

The Santa Claus Parade

Music and Lyrics by Johnny Marks

Strum Pattern: 4
Pick Pattern: 3

1. There's a (2.) hap - py cel - e - bra - tion in each town a - cross the na - tion at the

San - ta Claus Pa - rade. _____ All the grown - ups and the

kid - dies in the towns and in the cit - ies love the San - ta Claus Pa -

rade. _____ Dash - er, Dan - cer, Pran - cer, Vix - en, Com - et, Cu - pid, Don - ner,

Blitz - en, Ru - dolph leads the whole bri - gade. _____ When you

To Coda ⊕

hear all the cheer - ing you will see San - ta near - ing at the San - ta

Interlude

Claus Pa - rade. _____ Clowns come tum - bling

all a - long the way as ev - 'ry band be - gins to play: "To all a

hap - py hol - i - day." And when you see the pres - ents load - ed in the

sleigh, you'll know that Christ - mas is - n't ver - y far a - way. _____ 2. There's a

⊕ *Coda*

Claus Pa - rade. _____

The Seven Blessings of Mary

Adaption and Arrangement by Ronnie Gilbert, Lee Hays, Fred Hellerman and Pete Seeger

Strum Pattern: 4
Pick Pattern: 3

1. The ver - y first bless-ing that Mar - y had, — it was the bless-ing of one, to
2. - 6. *See Additional Lyrics*

think that her son, Je - sus, was God's on - ly son, was God's on - ly was God's on - ly

Chorus

son. Come all ye to the wil - der - ness! Glo - ry, glo - ry be!

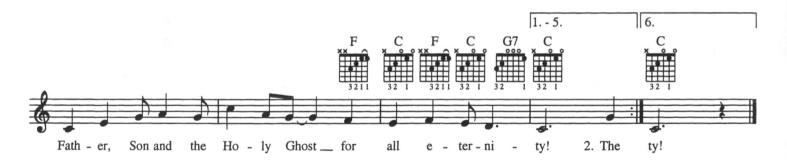

Fath - er, Son and the Ho - ly Ghost — for all e - ter - ni - ty! 2. The ty!

Additional Lyrics

2. The very next blessing that Mary had.
It was the blessing of two.
To think that her son,
Jesus could read the Bible through,
Could read the Bible through.

3. The very last blessing that Mary had,
It was the blessing of three,
To think that her son,
Jesus could make the blind to see.
Could make the blind to see.

4. The very next blessing that Mary had,
It was the blessing of four,
To think that her son Jesus
Would live to help the poor.
Would live to help the poor.

5. Now, Mary had these blessings,
She counted one by one.
She knew the greatest blessing.
Was her godly son.
Was her godly son.

6. The very last blessing that Mary had,
It was the blessing of seven,
To know that her son Jesus
Was safe at last in Heav'n,
Was safe at last in Heav'n.

Shepherd's Cradle Song

Words and Music by C.D. Schubert

Strum Pattern: 8
Pick Pattern: 8

Verse
Moderately Slow

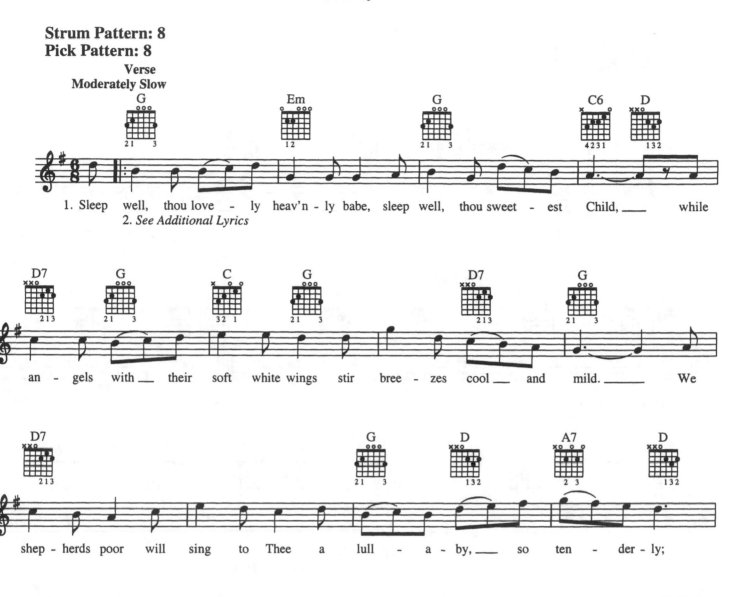

1. Sleep well, thou love - ly heav'n - ly babe, sleep well, thou sweet - est Child, ___ while
2. See Additional Lyrics

an - gels with __ their soft white wings stir bree - zes cool __ and mild. _____ We

shep - herds poor will sing to Thee a lull - a - by, ___ so ten - der - ly;

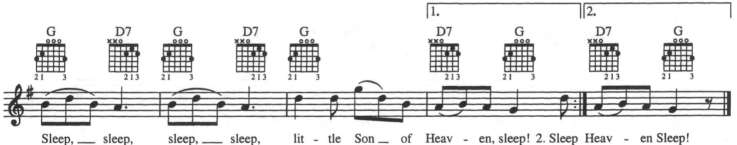

Sleep, __ sleep, sleep, __ sleep, lit - tle Son __ of Heav - en, sleep! 2. Sleep Heav - en Sleep!

Additional Lyrics

2. Sleep well while Mary holds Thee close,
   Sleep well upon her breast;
   Dear Joseph scarcely dares to breathe,
   He'd not disturbed Thy rest!
   The lambs stand mute about the stall
   As they adore Thee, Lord of All!
   Sleep, sleep.
   Little Son of Heaven, sleep!

Shout the Glad Tidings

Traditional

Strum Pattern: 7
Pick Pattern: 7

Silent Night

Words by Joseph Mohr
Translated by John F. Young
Music by Franz X. Gruber

Strum Pattern: 7
Pick Pattern: 9

Verse
Quietly

1. Si - lent night, ho - ly night! All is calm,
2., 3. *See Additional Lyrics*

all is bright. Round yon Vir - gin Moth - er and Child.

Ho - ly In - fant so ten - der and mild, sleep in heav - en - ly

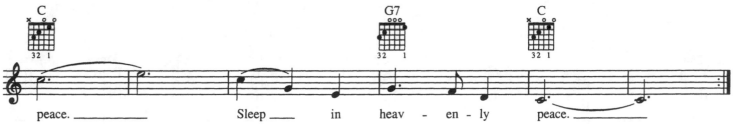

peace. _____ Sleep ___ in heav - en - ly peace. _____

Additional Lyrics

2. Silent night, holy night!
   Shepherds quake at the sight.
   Glories stream from heaven afar.
   Heavenly hosts sing Alleluia.
   Christ the Savior is born!
   Christ the Savior is born!

3. Silent night, holy night!
   Son of God, love's pure light.
   Radiant beams from thy holy face
   With the dawn of redeeming grace,
   Jesus Lord at Thy birth.
   Jesus Lord at Thy birth.

Silver and Gold

Music and Lyrics by Johnny Marks

Strum Pattern: 8
Pick Pattern: 8
Verse
Slowly And Expressively

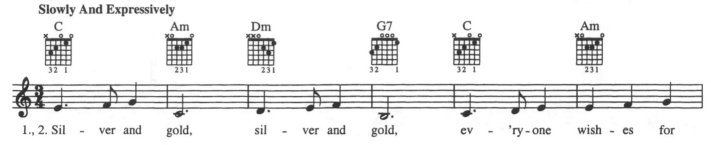

1., 2. Sil - ver and gold, sil - ver and gold, ev - 'ry-one wish - es for

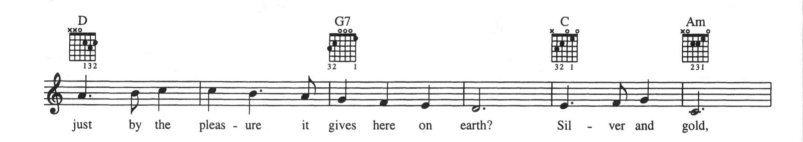

sil - ver and gold. How do you meas - ure its worth, _____

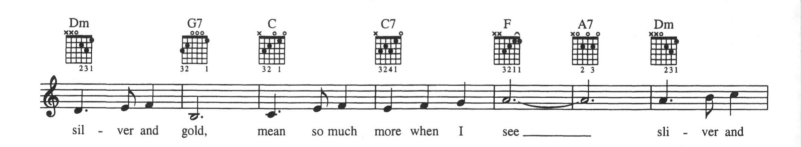

just by the pleas - ure it gives here on earth? Sil - ver and gold,

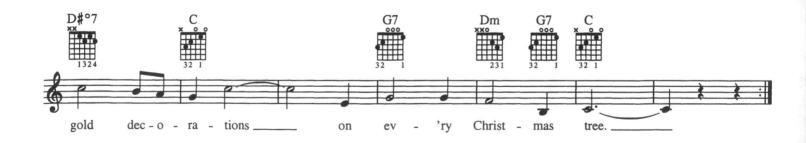

sil - ver and gold, mean so much more when I see _____ sli - ver and

gold dec - o - ra - tions _____ on ev - 'ry Christ - mas tree. _____

Silver Bells

from the Paramount Picture THE LEMON DROP KID
Words and Music by Jay Livingston and Ray Evans

Strum Pattern: 9
Pick Pattern: 8

Additional Lyrics

2. Strings of street lights, even stop lights
   Blink a bright red and green,
   As the shoppers rush home with their treasures.
   Hear the snow crunch, see the kids bunch,
   This is Santa's big scene,
   And above all the bustle you hear:

The Simple Birth

Traditional Flemish Carol

Strum Pattern: 8
Pick Pattern: 8

Verse
Moderately Slow

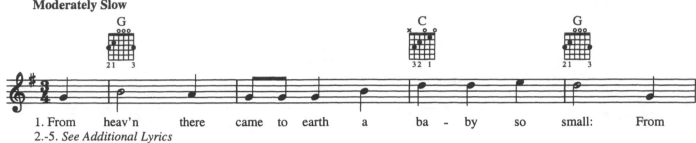

1. From heav'n there came to earth a ba - by so small: From
2.-5. *See Additional Lyrics*

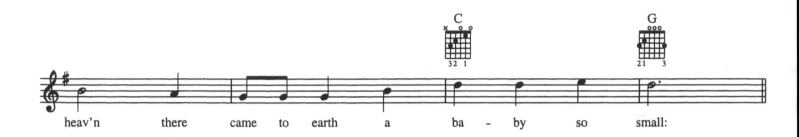

heav'n there came to earth a ba - by so small:

Chorus

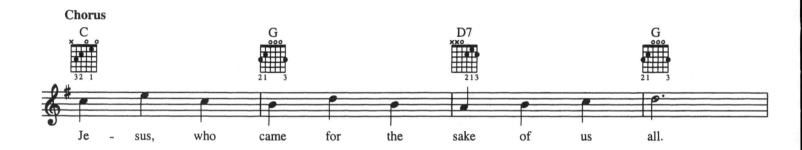

Je - sus, who came for the sake of us all.

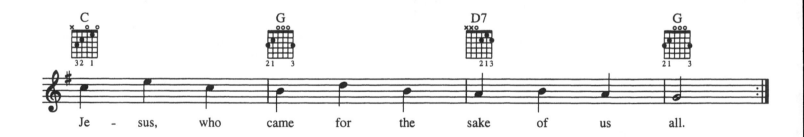

Je - sus, who came for the sake of us all.

Additional Lyrics

2. Beneath His tiny head no pillow but hay:
   Beneath His tiny head no pillow but hay:
   God's richest treasures in rude manger lay.
   God's richest treasures in rude manger lay.

3. His eyes of blackest jet were sparkling with light:
   His eyes of blackest jet were sparkling with light:
   Rosy cheeks bloomed on His face fair and bright.
   Rosy cheeks bloomed on His face fair and bright.

4. And from His lovely mouth, the laughter did swell:
   And from His lovely mouth, the laughter did swell:
   When He saw Mary, whom He loved so well.
   When He saw Mary, whom He loved so well.

5. He came to weary earth, so dark and so drear:
   He came to weary earth, so dark and so drear:
   To wish to mankind a blessed New Year.
   To wish to mankind a blessed New Year.

The Snow Lay on the Ground

Traditional Irish Carol

Strum Pattern: 7
Pick Pattern: 9

Verse
Slowly

1. The snow lay on the ground, the star shone bright when
2., 3. *See Additional Lyrics*

Christ our Lord was born on Christ - mas night. Ve – ni - te ad - o -

re – mus Do – mi – num; Ve – ni - te ad - o - re – mus

Chorus

Do – mi – num. Ve – ni - te ad - o - re – mus Do – mi –

num; Ve – ni - te ad - o - re – mus Do – mi – num.

Additional Lyrics

2. 'Twas Mary, virgin pure of Holy Anne
   That brought into this world the God made man.
   She laid him in a stall at Bethlehem.
   The ass and oxen share the roof with them.

3. Saint Joseph too, was by to tend the Child,
   To guard him and protect his mother mild.
   The angels hovered 'round and sang this song;
   Venite adoremus Dominum.

Snowfall

Lyrics by Ruth Thornhill
Music by Claude Thornhill

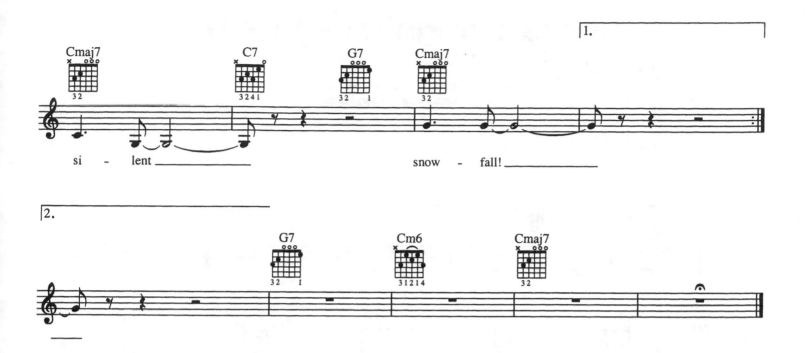

si - lent _____ snow - fall! _____

While Shepherds Watched Their Flocks

Words by Nahum Tate
Music by George Frideric Handel

Strum Pattern: 3
Pick Pattern: 3
   Verse
    Moderately

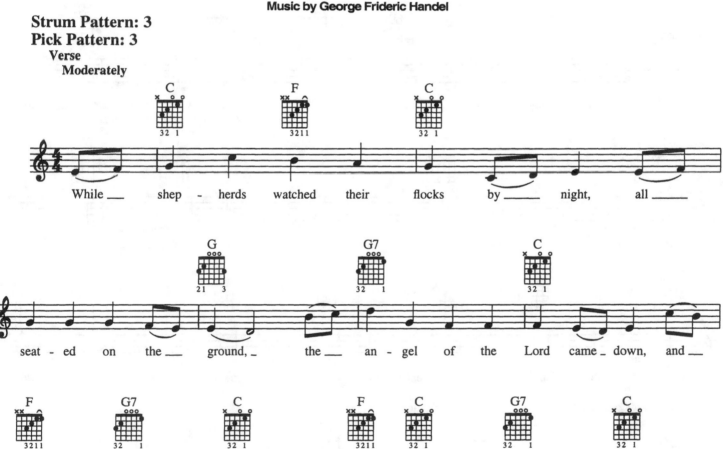

While ___ shep - herds watched their flocks by ___ night, all ___

seat - ed on the ___ ground, ___ the ___ an - gel of the Lord came ___ down, and ___

glo - ry shone a - round, ___ and glo - ry shone a - round.

Some Things for Christmas
(A Snake, Some Mice, Some Glue and a Hole Too)

Lyric by Jacquelyn Reinach and Joan Lamport
Music by Jacquelyn Reinach

© 1965 (Renewed) MPL COMMUNICATIONS, INC.

lots   I   can   do, _____   with   a   lit - tle   bit   of

glue _____   and   a   shoe! _____   3., 5. I'm

Verse

not   ask - ing   much   for   Christ - mas, _____   just   a   snake   and   some   mice   and   some

{ glue; _____   just   some   mice   and   a   snake   and   some   glue   sure   would   make }   my
{ glue _____   and   some   worms   and   some   fleas,   just   a   few   things   like   these 'd make }

2nd time, D.S. al Coda   ⊕ *Coda*

dreams   come   true!   ⎯

Additional Lyrics

4. I could use some worms for Christmas,
   All ooey and gooey and wet;
   Think of the squirms when Dad sees those worms,
   In a dish of meatballs and spaghet'!

Bridge And, if you please,
   If you purty purty please,
   For my brother's dungarees,
   Send me fleas!

6. I want a hole for Christmas,
   A hole that is deep as it's wide;
   When Mommy finds out what this song's about,
   Then I'll have a good place to hide!

Some Children See Him

Lyric by Wihla Hutson
Music by Alfred Burt

Strum Pattern: 7 & 10
Pick Pattern: 7 & 10

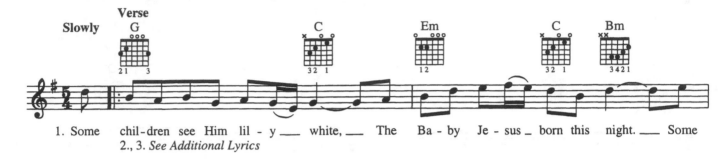

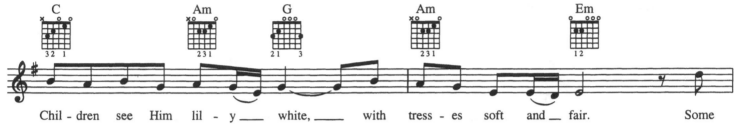

1. Some chil-dren see Him lil - y __ white, __ The Ba - by Je - sus __ born this night. __ Some
2., 3. *See Additional Lyrics*

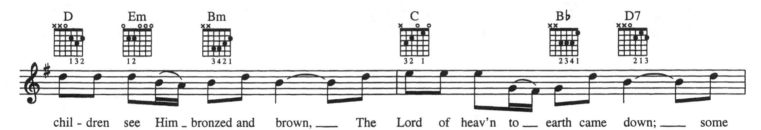

Chil - dren see Him lil - y __ white, __ with tress - es soft and __ fair. Some

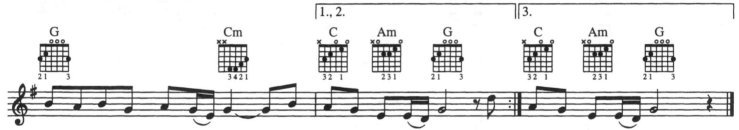

chil - dren see Him __ bronzed and brown, __ The Lord of heav'n to __ earth came down; __ some

chil-dren see Him bronzed and __ brown, __ with dark and heav - y __ hair. 2. Some love that's born to - night!

Additional Lyrics

2. Some children see Him almond eyed,
This Savior whom we kneel beside.
Some children see Him almond eyed,
With skin of yellow hue.
Some children see Him dark as they,
Sweet Mary's Son to whom we pray;
Some children see Him dark as they,
And ah! They love Him too!

3. The children in each diff'rent place
Will see the Baby Jesus' face
Like theirs, but bright with heav'nly grace;
And filled with holy light.
O lay aside each earthly thing,
And with thy heart as offering,
Come worship now the infant King,
'Tis love that's born tonight!

Standing in the Rain

Words and Music by Sydney Carter

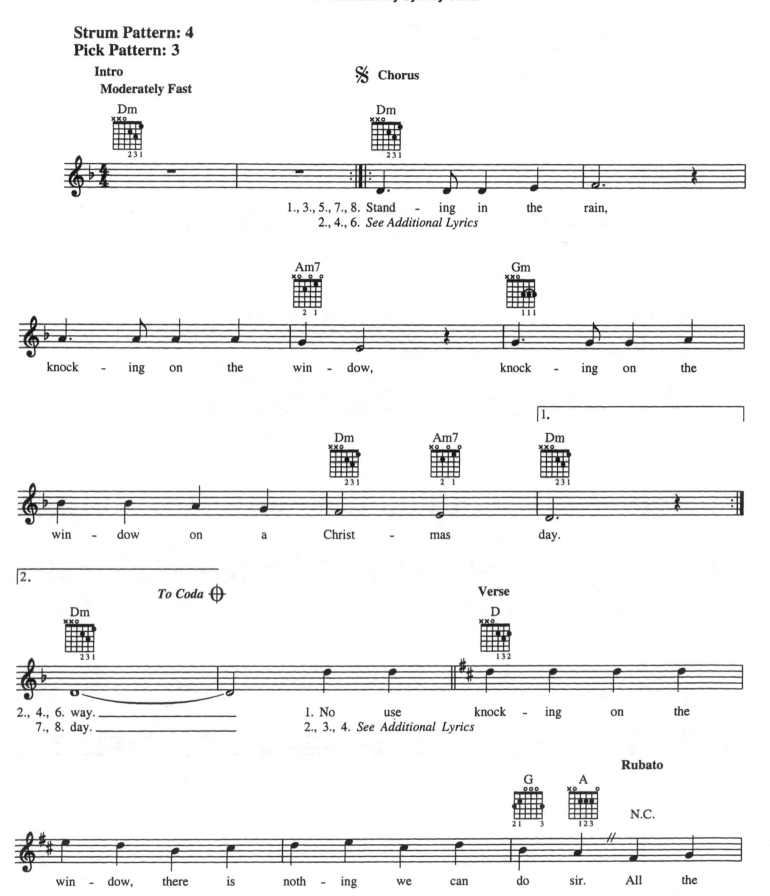

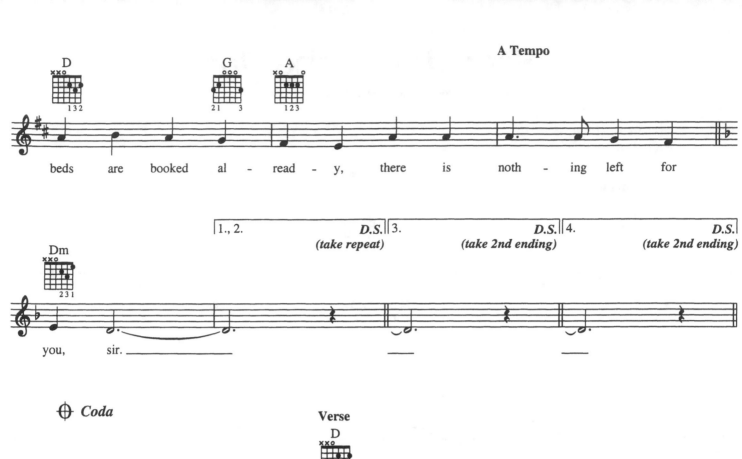

A Tempo

beds are booked al - read - y, there is noth - ing left for

1., 2.   D.S. | 3.   D.S. | 4.   D.S.
(take repeat)   (take 2nd ending)   (take 2nd ending)

you, sir. _____

Coda   Verse

_____ 5. Wish - ing you a mer - ry Christ - mas we will

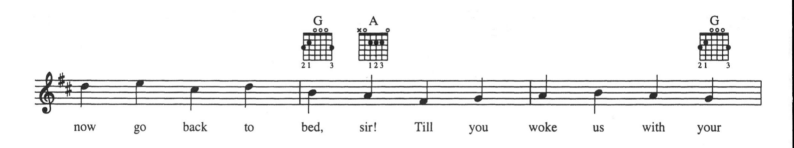

now go back to bed, sir! Till you woke us with your

A Tempo

knock - ing we were sleep - ing like the dead, sir. _____

Outro-Chorus

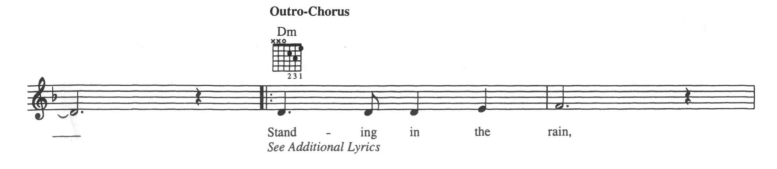

Stand - ing in the rain,
See Additional Lyrics

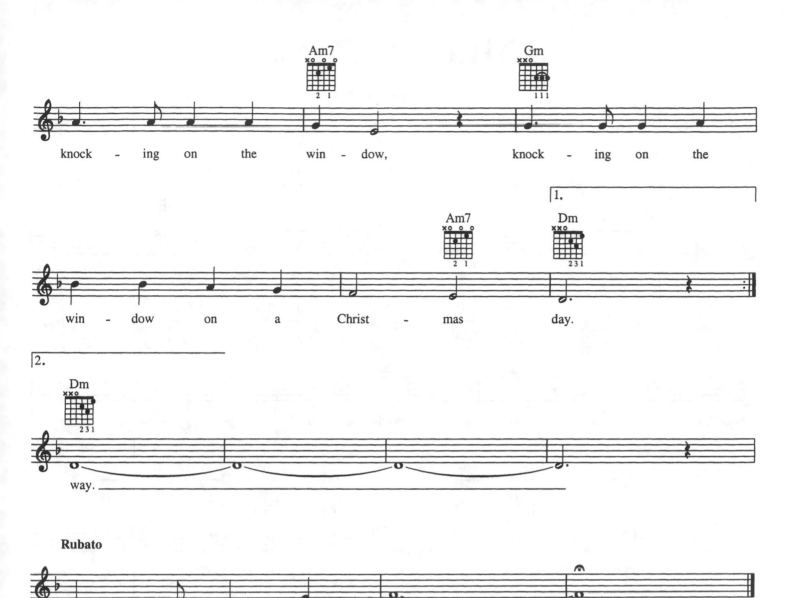

knock - ing on the win - dow, knock - ing on the

win - dow on a Christ - mas day.

way.

Rubato

Stand - ing in the rain.

Additional Lyrics

Chorus 2., 4., 6. There he is again,
      Knocking on the window,
      Knocking on the window in the same old way.

2. No use knocking on the window;
   Some are lucky, some are not, sir.
   We are Christian men and women,
   But we're keeping what we've got, sir.

3. No, we haven't got a manger,
   No, we haven't got a stable.
   We are Christian men and women
   Always willing, never able.

4. Jesus Christ has gone to heaven,
   One day he'll be coming back, sir.
   In this house he will be welcome.
   But we hope he won't be black, sir.

Outro-Chorus There he is again,
      Knocking on the window,
      Knocking on the window in the same old way.
      Standing in the rain.

The Star Carol

Lyric by Wihla Hutson
Music by Alfred Burt

Strum Pattern: 8
Pick Pattern: 8

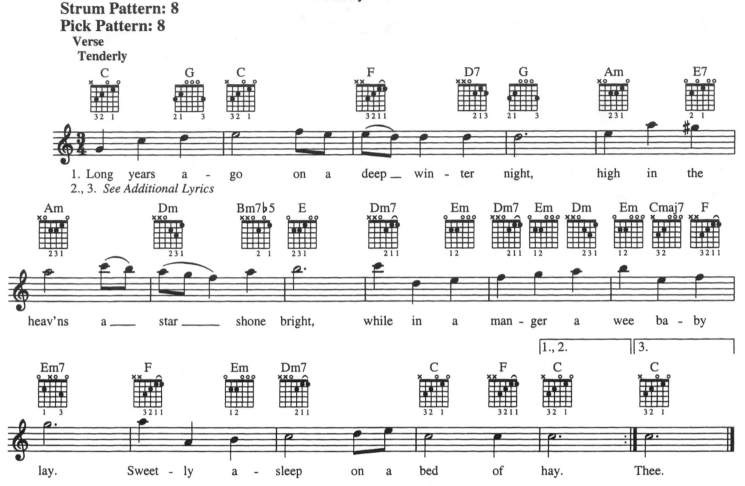

1. Long years a-go on a deep win-ter night, high in the
2., 3. *See Additional Lyrics*

heav'ns a star shone bright, while in a man-ger a wee ba-by

lay. Sweet-ly a-sleep on a bed of hay. Thee.

Additional Lyrics

2. Jesus, the Lord was that Baby so small,
Laid down to sleep in a humble stall;
Then came the star and it stood overhead,
Shedding its light 'round His little bed.

3. Dear Baby Jesus, how tiny Thou art,
I'll make a place for Thee in my heart,
And when the stars in the heavens I see,
Ever and always I'll think of Thee.

The Star Carol
(Canzone D'i Zampognari)

English Lyric and Music Adaptation by Peter Seeger
(Based on a Traditional Neapolitan Carol)

Strum Pattern: 8
Pick Pattern: 8

Brightly

1. 'Twas on a night like this, _____ a lit-tle
bove them shone a star, _____ a star so

D

Babe ___ was born; _____ the shep - herds gath - ered 'round _____
won - d'rous light; _____ nev - er since in all these years _____

G C G D7 G |1. **G** |2.

___ to _____ guard Him till the dawn. 2. A bright.
___ have we seen one half so

Chorus

G D G

Shin - ing so tru - ly, shin - ing so bright - ly, guid - ing { 1. their }
{ 2. our }

D G

foot - steps from ___ a - far. _____ It { 1. led } them through ___ the
{ 2. leads } us

D

night, _____ a path to love and broth - er - hood _____ by ___

To Coda ⊕   **D.S. al Coda**   ⊕ *Coda*
                (take repeat)

G C G D7 G   **G**

fol - low - ing its light. _____ 3. Oh,   light. _____

Additional Lyrics

3. Oh, come with us tonight,
   And join us on our way;
   For we have found that star once more
   To greet a better day.

4. For though through out our land
   Men search the skies in vain,
   Yet turn their glance within their hearts
   They would find this star again.

225

The Star of Christmas Morning

Traditional

Strum Pattern: 8
Pick Pattern: 8

Verse
Moderately Slow

We saw a light shine out a - far, on Christ - mas in the morn - ing. And straight we knew it was Christ's star, bright beam - ing in the morn - ing. Then did we fall on bend - ed knee, on Christ - mas in the morn - ing. And praise the Lord, who'd let us see His glo - ry at its dawn - ing.

Star of the East

Words by George Cooper
Music by Amanda Kennedy

Strum Pattern: 9
Pick Pattern: 9

Still, Still, Still

Salzburg Melody, c.1819
Traditional Austrian Text

Strum Pattern: 4
Pick Pattern: 3

Verse
Moderately Slow

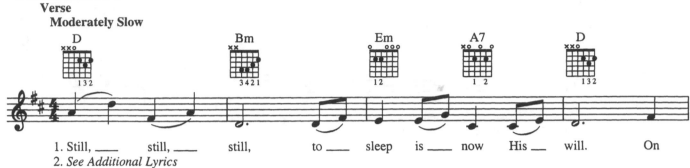

1. Still, ___ still, ___ still, to ___ sleep is ___ now His ___ will. On
2. *See Additional Lyrics*

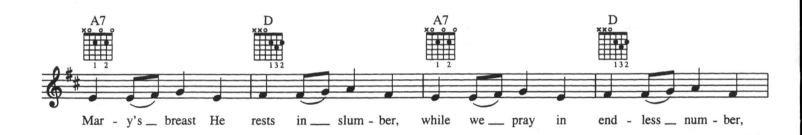

Mar - y's ___ breast He rests in ___ slum - ber, while we ___ pray in end - less ___ num - ber,

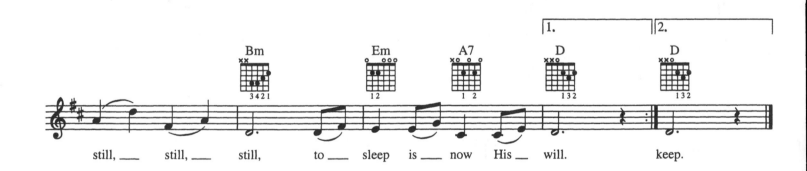

still, ___ still, ___ still, to ___ sleep is ___ now His ___ will. keep.

Additional Lyrics

2. Sleep, sleep, sleep, while we Thy vigil keep.
And angels come from Heaven singing,
Songs of jubilation bringing,
Sleep, sleep, sleep, while we Thy vigil keep.

Suzy Snowflake

Words and Music by Sid Tepper and Roy Bennett

Strum Pattern: 3
Pick Pattern: 3

Tennessee Christmas

Words and Music by Amy Grant and Gary Chapman

love cir - cles a - round ___ us like the gifts ___ a - round ___ our tree. ___

1. Well, I know (3.) there's more snow ___ up in Co - lo - ra - do than my roof ___
2. Well, they say ___ in L. A. ___ it's a warm ___ hol - i - day it's the on -

___ will ev - er see. ___ }
- ly place ___ to be. ___ }

But a ten - der Ten - nes - see Christ - mas is the

To Coda ✛   1.   2.   *D.S. al Coda*

on - ly Christ - mas for me.   me.   3. Well, I know ___

✛ *Coda*

me.   A ten - der Ten - nes - see Christ - mas is the on - ly

Christ - mas for me.

Additional Lyrics

2. Ev'ry now and then I get a wanderin' urge to see,
Maybe California, maybe tinsel town's for me.
There's a parade there, we'd have it made there.
Bring home a tan for New Year's Eve.
Sure sounds exciting, awfully inviting.
Still I think I'm gonna keep...

That Christmas Feeling

Words and Music by Bennie Benjamin and George Weiss

Strum Pattern: 3
Pick Pattern: 3
Verse
Moderately Slow

There's a Song in the Air

Words and Music by Josiah G. Holland and Karl P. Harrington

Strum Pattern: 8
Pick Pattern: 8
Verse
Moderately Fast

1. There's a song in the air! There's a star in the sky! There's a
2., 3., 4. *See Additional Lyrics*

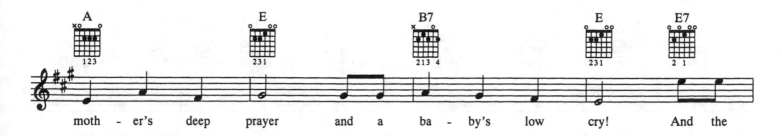

moth - er's deep prayer and a ba - by's low cry! And the

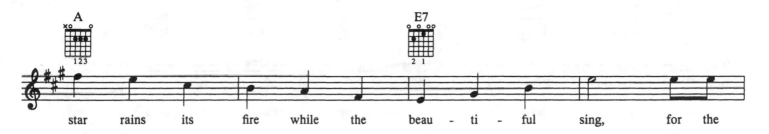

star rains its fire while the beau - ti - ful sing, for the

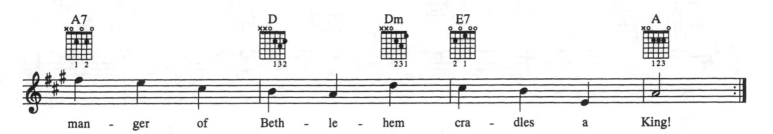

man - ger of Beth - le - hem cra - dles a King!

Additional Lyrics

2. There's a tumult of joy o'er the wonderful birth,
   For the Virgin's sweet boy is the lord of the earth.
   Ay! The star rains its fire while the beautiful sing,
   For the manger of Bethlehem cradles a King!

3. In the light of that star lie the ages impearled,
   And that song from afar has swept over the world.
   Ev'ry hearth is a flame and the beautiful sing
   In the homes of the nations that Jesus is King!

4. We rejoice in the light and we echo the song
   That comes down thro' the night from the heavenly throng.
   Ay! we should to the lovely Evangel they bring,
   And we greet in his cradle, our Savior and King!

This Is Christmas
(Bright, Bright the Holly Berries)

Lyric by Wihla Hutson
Music by Alfred Burt

Strum Pattern: 7, 8
Pick Pattern: 7, 9
Verse
Liltingly

1. Bright, bright the hol-ly ber-ries in the wreath up-on the door.
2., 3. *See Additional Lyrics*

Bright, bright the hap-py fac-es with the thoughts of joys in store.

White, white the snow-y mead-ow wrapped in slum-ber deep and sweet.

White, white the mis-tle-toe ___ 'neath which two lov-ers meet.

Chorus

This is Christ-mas, this is Christ-mas, this is Christ-mas time. ___

Additional Lyrics

2. Gay, gay the children's voices filled with laughter, filled with glee.
Gay, gay the tinsled things upon the dark and spicy tree.
Day, day when all mankind may hear the angel's song again.
Day, day when Christ was born to bless the sons of men.

3. Sing, sing ye heav'nly host to tell the blessed Saviour's birth.
Sing, sing in holy joy, ye dwellers all upon the earth.
King, King yet tiny Babe, come down to us from God above.
King, King of ev'ry heart which opens wide to love.

'Twas the Night Before Christmas

Words by Clement Clark Moore
Music by F. Henri Klickman

Strum Pattern: 4
Pick Pattern: 5

Verse
Brightly

1. 'Twas the night be-fore Christ-mas, when all through the house, not a crea-ture was stir-ring, not e - ven a mouse. The
2.-7. *See Additional Lyrics*

stock-ings were hung by the chim-ney with care, In hopes that Saint Nich - o - las soon would be there. The

chil-dren were nest - led all snug in their beds, while vis-ions of su - gar plums danced through their heads. And

Ma-ma in her 'ker - chief and I in my cap, Had just set - tled our brains for a long win-ter's nap.

Additional Lyrics

2. When out on the lawn there arouse such a clatter;
I sprang from my bed to see what was the matter.
Away to the window I flew like a flash,
Tore open the shutters and threw up the sash.
The moon, on the breast of the new-fallen snow,
Gave a lustre of midday to objects below.
When what to my wondering eyes should appear.
But a miniature sleigh and eight tiny reindeer.

3. With a little old driver; so lively and quick,
I knew in a moment it must be Saint Nick.
More rapid than eagles, his coursers they came
And he whistled, and shouted, and called them by name;
"Now, Dasher, Now, Dancer! Now, Prancer! Now, Vixen!
On Comet! On, Cupid! On Donder and Blitzen!
To the top of the porch, to the top of the wall!
Now dash away, dash away, dash away all!"

4. As dry leaves that before the wild hurricane fly,
When they meet with an obstacle, mount to the sky.
So up to the house-top the coursers they flew,
With the sleigh full of toys, and Saint Nicholas, too.
And then in a twinkling I heard on the roof
The prancing and pawing of each little hoof.
As I drew in my head, and was turning around,
Down the chimney Saint Nicholas came with a bound.

5. He was dressed all in fir from his head to his foot
And his clothes were all tarnished with ashes and soot.
And he looked like a peddler just opening his pack.
His eyes how they twinkled! His dimples how merry!
His cheeks were like roses, his nose like a cherry,
His droll little mouth was drawn up like a bow
And the beard of his chin was as white as the snow.

6. The stump of a pipe he held tight in his teeth
And the smoke, it encircled his head like a wreath.
He had a broad face, and a round little belly
That shook, when he laughed, like a bowl full of jelly.
He was chubby and plump, a right jolly old elf,
And I laughed when I saw him, in spite of myself.
A wink of his eye and a twist of his head,
Soon gave me to know I had nothing to dread.

7. He spake not a word but went straight to his work,
And filled all the stockings, then turned with a jerk,
And laying his finger aside of his nose,
And giving a nod, up the chimney he rose.
He sprang to his sleigh, to his team gave a whistle,
And away they all flew like the down of a thistle,
But I heard him exclaim, ere he drove out of sight:
"Happy Christmas to all, and all a Good-night!"

This One's for the Children

Words and Music by Maurice Starr

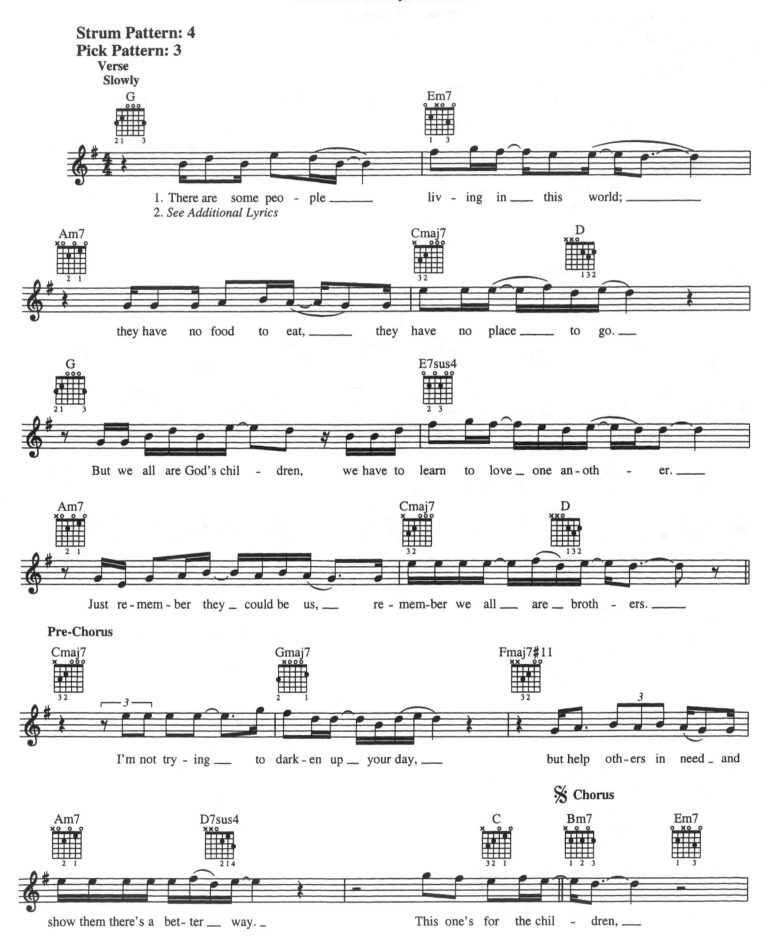

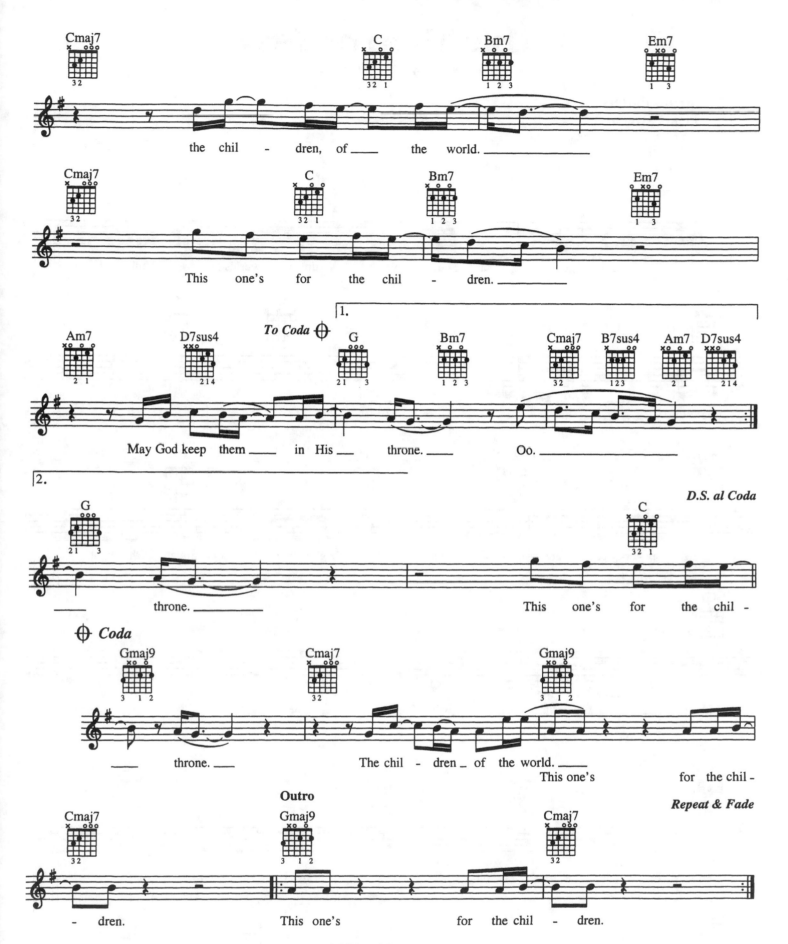

Additional Lyrics

2. Many people are happy
   And many people are sad.
   Some people have many things
   That others can only wish they had.
   So, for the sake of the children,
   Show them love's the only way to go
   'Cause they're our tomorrow,
   And people they've got to know.

This Time of Year

Words and Music by Cliff Owens and Jesse Hollis

San-ta Claus is on his way __ with loads of joy on his sleigh

1.

this time _____ of the year when Christ-mas is near.

2.

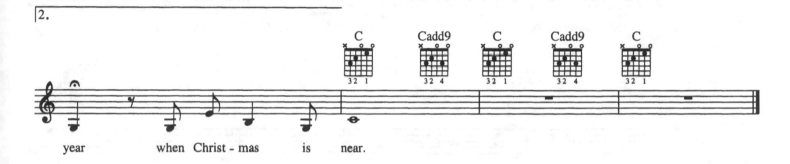

year when Christ - mas is near.

Toyland

from BABES IN TOYLAND

Words by Glen MacDonough
Music by Victor Herbert

Strum Pattern: 9
Pick Pattern: 9

Verse
Slowly

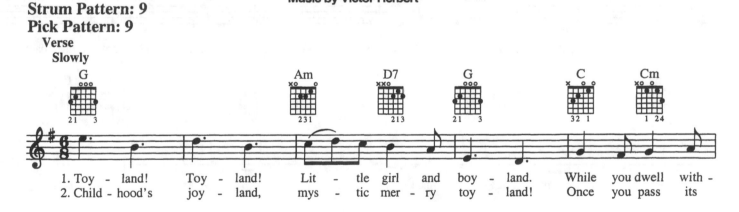

1. Toy - land! Toy - land! Lit - tle girl and boy - land. While you dwell with -
2. Child - hood's joy - land, mys - tic mer - ry toy - land! Once you pass its

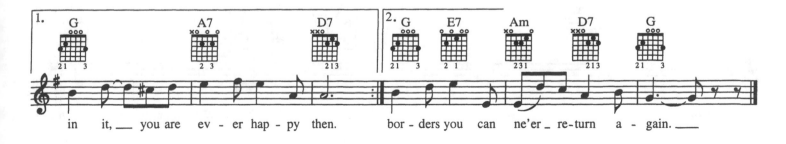

1. in it, __ you are ev - er hap - py then.   **2.** bor - ders you can ne'er __ re - turn a - gain. __

Three Wise Men, Wise Men Three

Words and Music by Gloria Shayne and Noel Regney

The Twelve Days of Christmas

Traditional English Carol

Strum Pattern: 3
Pick Pattern: 3

Verse
Moderately

1. On the first day of Christ - mas, my true love gave to me: a par - tridge _ in a pear

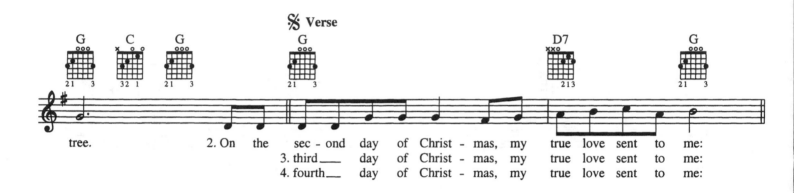

tree.
2. On the sec - ond day of Christ - mas, my true love sent to me:
3. third ___ day of Christ - mas, my true love sent to me:
4. fourth ___ day of Christ - mas, my true love sent to me:

Repeat as needed

D.S. for Verses 3. & 4.

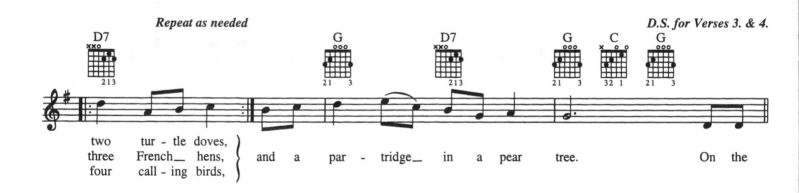

two   tur - tle doves,
three   French _ hens,   and a par - tridge _ in a pear tree.   On the
four   call - ing birds,

Verse

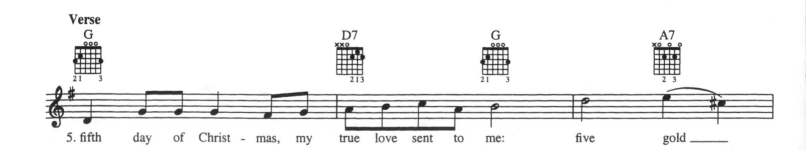

5. fifth   day of Christ - mas, my true love sent to me: five   gold _____

Pick Pattern: 8
Strum Pattern: 8

rings. Four ___ call - ing birds, three French hens,

Pick Pattern: 3
Strum Pattern: 3

12th Verse, To Coda ⊕

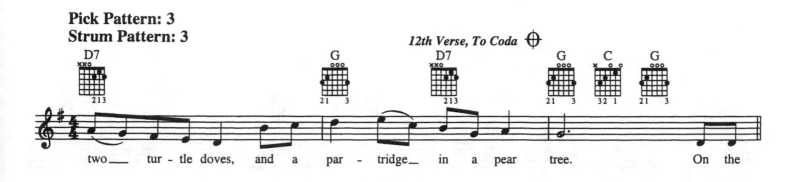

two ___ tur - tle doves, and a par - tridge ___ in a pear tree. On the

Verse

6. sixth ___ day of Christ - mas, my true love sent to me:
7. sev - enth day of Christ - mas, my true love sent to me:
8. eighth ___ day of Christ - mas, my true love sent to me:
9. ninth ___ day of Christ - mas, my true love sent to me:
10. tenth ___ day of Christ - mas, my true love sent to me:
11. 'lev - enth day of Christ - mas, my true love sent to me:
12. twelfth ___ day of Christ - mas, my true love sent to me:

Repeat as needed　　　　　　　　*D.S.S. for Verses 7.-12.*　　　⊕ *Coda*

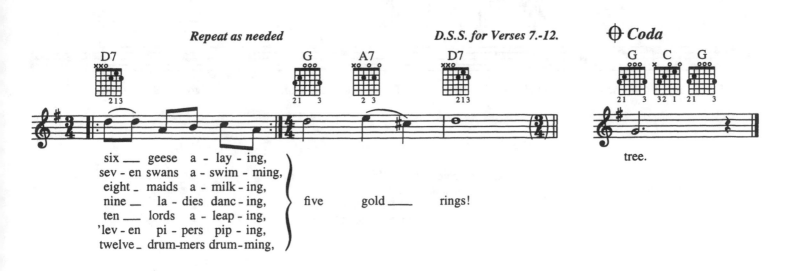

six ___ geese a - lay - ing,
sev - en swans a - swim - ming,
eight ___ maids a - milk - ing,
nine ___ la - dies danc - ing, } five gold ___ rings!
ten ___ lords a - leap - ing,
'lev - en pi - pers pip - ing,
twelve ___ drum-mers drum - ming,

tree.

Up on the Housetop

Words and Music by B.R. Handy

Strum Pattern: 4, 3
Pick Pattern: 5, 3

Verse
Brightly

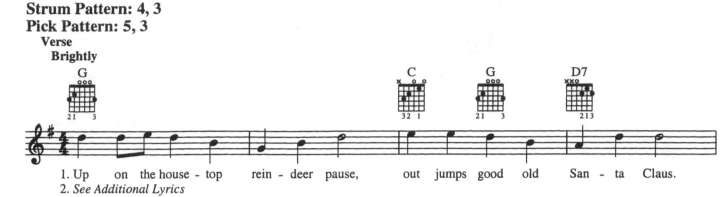

1. Up on the house - top rein - deer pause, out jumps good old San - ta Claus.
2. *See Additional Lyrics*

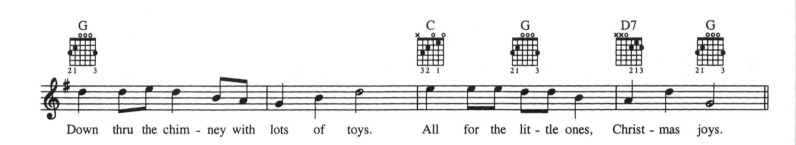

Down thru the chim - ney with lots of toys. All for the lit - tle ones, Christ - mas joys.

Chorus

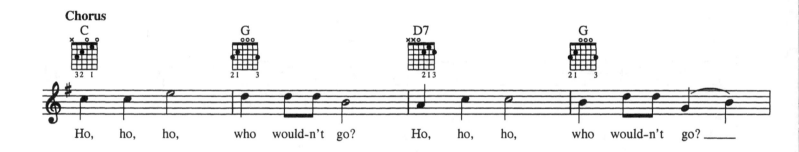

Ho, ho, ho, who would-n't go? Ho, ho, ho, who would-n't go? _____

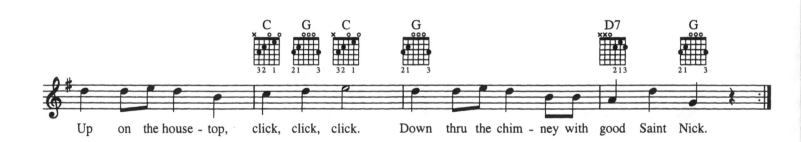

Up on the house - top, click, click, click. Down thru the chim - ney with good Saint Nick.

Additional Lyrics

2. First comes the stocking of Little Nell,
Oh, dear Santa, fill it well.
Give her a dollie that laughs and cries,
One that will open and shut her eyes.

A Virgin Unspotted

Traditional English Carol

Strum Pattern: 8
Pick Pattern: 8

1. A virgin unspotted, the prophet foretold, should bring forth a Savior, which we now behold; to be our Redeemer from death, hell, and sin, which Adam's transgression had wrapped us in. Aye, and therefore be merry, set sorrow aside, Christ Jesus, our Savior, was born on this tide.

2., 3., 4. *See Additional Lyrics*

Chorus

1., 2., 3. | 4.

2. Then tide.

Additional Lyrics

2. Then God sent an angel from Heaven so high,
   To certain poor shepherds in fields where they lie,
   And bade them no longer in sorrow to stay,
   Because that our Savior was born on this day.

3. Then presently after, the shepherds did spy
   Vast numbers of angels to stand in the sky;
   They joyfully talked and sweetly did sing:
   "To God be all glory, our heavenly King."

4. To teach us humility all this was done,
   And learn we form thence haughty pride for to shun;
   A manger His cradle who came from above,
   The great God of mercy, of peace and of love.

Watchman, Tell Us of the Night

Traditional

Strum Pattern: 4
Pick Pattern: 3

1. Watch - man tell us of the night, what its signs of prom - ise are.
2.,3. *See Additional Lyrics*

Trav - 'ler o'er yon moun - tain's height, see that glo - ry beam - ing star.

Watch - man does __ its beau - teous ray aught of joy or hope for - tell?

Trav - 'ler, yes, it brings the day, prom - ised day of Is - ra - el. God is come.

Additional Lyrics

2. Watchman, tell us of the night,
   Higher yet that star ascends.
   Trav'ler, blessedness and light,
   Peace and truth, its course portends.
   Watchman, will its beams alone
   Gild the spot that gave them birth!
   Trav'ler, ages are its own;
   See it bursts o'er all the earth.

3. Watchman, tell us of the night,
   For the morning seems to dawn.
   Trav'ler, darkness takes its flight;
   Doubt and terror are withdrawn.
   Watchman, let thy wanderings cease;
   Hie thee to thy quiet home!
   Trav'ler, lo, the Prince of Peace,
   Lo, the Son of God is come.

We Are Santa's Elves

Music and Lyrics by Johnny Marks

Strum Pattern: 3
Pick Pattern: 3

Additional Lyrics

2. We work hard all day.
   But our work is play.
   Dolls we try out,
   See if they cry out
   We are Santa's elves.

3. Santa knows who's good.
   Do the things you should.
   And we bet you
   He won't forget you.
   We are Santa's elves.

We Need a Little Christmas

from MAME

Music and Lyric by Jerry Herman

Strum Pattern: 4
Pick Pattern: 1

Verse
Brightly

1. Haul out the hol - ly. _____ Put up the
2. *See Additional Lyrics*

tree be - fore my spir - it falls _____ a - gain.

Fill up the stock - ing. _____ I may be

rush - ing things, but deck the halls _____ a - gain

now. _____ For we
3. For we

need a lit - tle Christ - mas, right this ver - y min - ute,
need a lit - tle mu - sic, need a lit - tle laugh - ter,

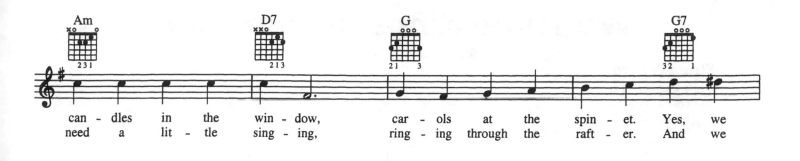

can - dles in the win - dow, car - ols at the spin - et. Yes, we
need a lit - tle sing - ing, ring - ing through the raft - er. And we

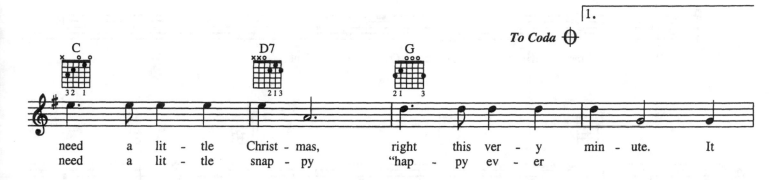

1.

To Coda ✛

need a lit - tle Christ - mas, right this ver - y min - ute. It
need a lit - tle snap - py "hap - py ev - er

has - n't snowed a sin - gle flur - ry, but San - ta, dear, we're in a hur - ry. 2. So

2.

D.S. al Coda

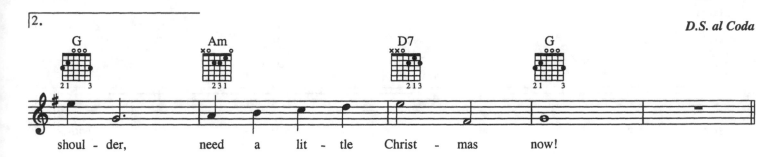

shoul - der, need a lit - tle Christ - mas now!

✛ *Coda*

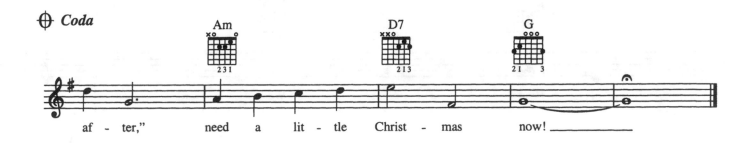

af - ter," need a lit - tle Christ - mas now! _____

Additional Lyrics

2. So climb down the chimney,
Turn on the brightest string of lights I've ever seen.
Slice up the fruitcake.
It's time we hung some tinsel on the evergreen bough.
For I've grown a little leaner, grown a little colder,
Grown a little sadder, grown a little older,
And I need a little angel, sitting on my shoulder,
Need a little Christmas now!

We Three Kings of Orient Are

Words and Music by John H. Hopkins, Jr.

Strum Pattern: 8
Pick Pattern: 8

We Wish You a Merry Christmas

Traditional English Folksong

Strum Pattern: 8, 9
Pick Pattern: 8, 9

Additional Lyrics

2. We all know that Santa's coming.
   We all know that Santa's coming.
   We all know that Santa's coming
   And soon will be here.

We'll Dress the House

Lyric by Wihla Hutson
Music by Alfred Burt

Strum Pattern: 8
Pick Pattern: 8

1. We'll dress the house with hol-ly bright and sprigs of mis-tle-toe;_____ we'll
2., 3. *See Additional Lyrics*

trim the Christ-mas tree to-night and set the lights a-glow;_____ we'll

wrap our gifts with rib-bons gay and give them out on Christ-mas Day; by

ev-'ry-thing we do and say, our glad-ness we will show.____ 2. We'll morn.____

Additional Lyrics

2. We'll dress the table daintily,
   Our finest treasures use,
   That all a-sparkle it may be
   And bright with lovely hues;
   Then for the feasting we'll prepare
   A kitchen full of wondrous fare,
   That each from all the dishes rare,
   His fav'rite one may choose.

3. And ye who would the Christ Child
   Greet Your heart also adorn,
   That it may be a dwelling meet
   For Him who now is born.
   Let all unlovely things give place
   To souls bedecked with heav'nly grace,
   That ye may view His Holy face,
   With joy on Christmas morn.

What Child Is This?

16th Century English Melody
Words by William C. Dix

Strum Pattern: 8, 7
Pick Pattern: 8, 9
Verse
Slow And Serene

1. What Child is this, ___ who, laid to rest, ___ on Ma - ry's
2. *See Additional Lyrics*

lap ___ is sleep - ing? Whom an - gels greet ___ with an - thems sweet ___ while

Chorus

shep - herds watch ___ are keep - ing? This, this ___ is Christ the
See Additional Lyrics

King, ___ whom shep - herds guard ___ and an - gels sing: Haste,

haste ___ to bring him laud, ___ the Babe, ___ the Son ___ of Ma - ry.

Additional Lyrics

2. So bring Him incense, gold and myrrh,
Come peasant king to own Him;
The King of kings salvation brings.
Let loving hearts enthrone Him,

Chorus Raise, raise the song on high,
The Virgin sings her lullaby;
Joy, joy for Christ is born,
The Babe, the Son of Mary.

What Are You Doing New Year's Eve?

By Frank Loesser

Strum Pattern: 5
Pick Pattern: 5

Verse
Moderately

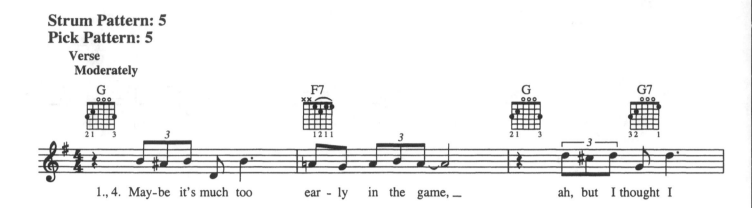

1., 4. May-be it's much too early in the game, — ah, but I thought I

ask you just the same, — what are you do-ing new year's, New Year's

Verse

Eve? 2., 5. Won-der whose arms will hold you good and tight, —

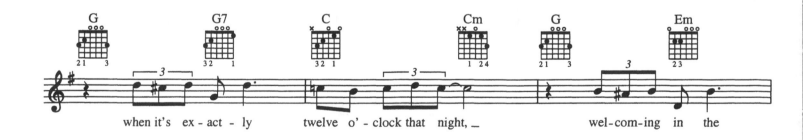

when it's ex-act-ly twelve o'-clock that night, — wel-com-ing in the

What Can You Get
a Wookie for Christmas
(When He Already Has a Comb)

Words and Music by Maury Yeston

Strum Pattern: 4
Pick Pattern: 3

Verse
Freely

257

When Christ Was Born of Mary Free

Traditional English Carol

Strum Pattern: 3, 4
Pick Pattern: 3, 4

1. When Christ was born of __ Mar - y __ free, in Beth - le - hem that fair cit - y.
2., 3. *See Additional Lyrics*

an - gels sang there with mirth and glee: "In ex - cel - sis __ glo - ri - a."

Chorus

In ex - cel - sis glo - ri - a, in ex - cel - sis glo - ri - a,

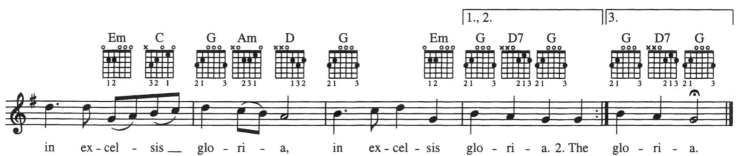

in ex - cel - sis __ glo - ri - a, in ex - cel - sis glo - ri - a. 2. The glo - ri - a.

Additional Lyrics

2. The King is come to save mankind,
   As in the scripture truths we find.
   Therefore this song we have in mind,
   "In excelsis gloria."

3. Then, dearest Lord, for Thy great grace,
   Grant us in bliss to see Thy face,
   That we may sing to Thy solace,
   "In excelsis gloria."

What Made the Baby Cry?

Words and Music by William J. Golay

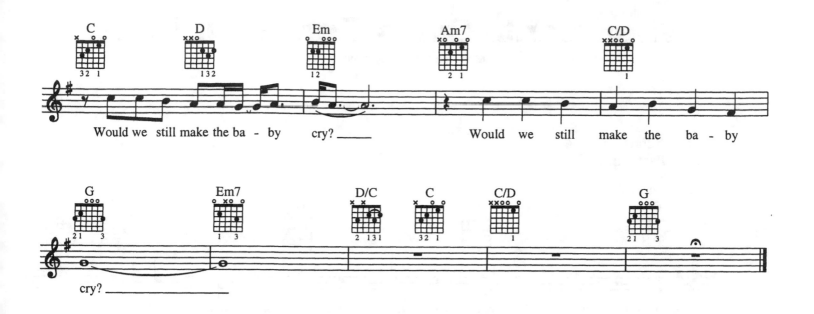

Would we still make the ba - by cry? ____ Would we still make the ba - by

cry? _____

Winds Through the Olive Trees

19th Century American Carol

Strum Pattern: 7
Pick Pattern: 7
Verse
Slowly

Winds through the ol - ive trees, soft - ly did blow, 'round lit - tle

Beth - le - hem, long, long a - go. Sheep on the hill - side lay

whit - er than snow, shep - herds were watch - ing them, long, long a - go.

When Santa Claus Gets Your Letter

Music and Lyrics by Johnny Marks

Strum Pattern: 3, 4
Pick Pattern: 3, 5

Intro
Moderately

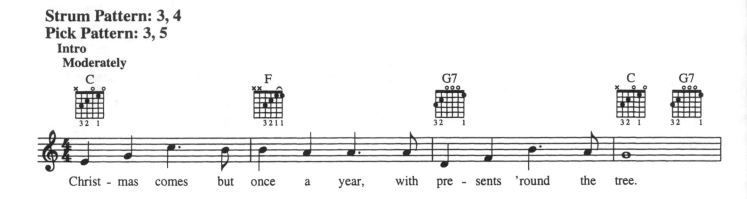

Christ - mas comes but once a year, with pre - sents 'round the tree.

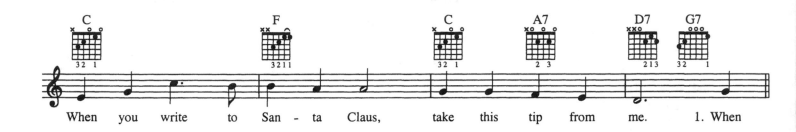

When you write to San - ta Claus, take this tip from me. 1. When

Verse

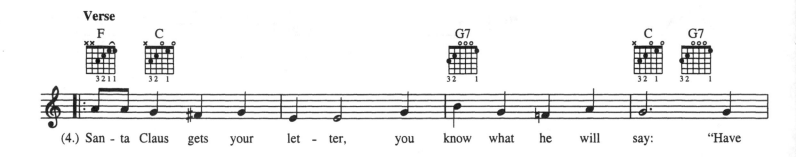

(4.) San - ta Claus gets your let - ter, you know what he will say: "Have

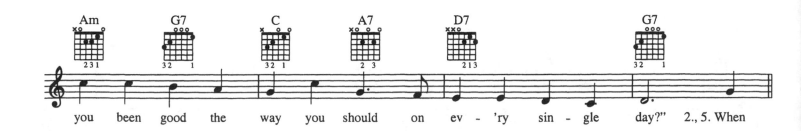

you been good the way you should on ev - 'ry sin - gle day?" 2., 5. When

Verse

Santa Claus gets your letter, to ask for Christmas toys, he'll take a look in his good book he keeps for girls and boys. He'll

Bridge

stroke his beard, his eyes will glow and at your name he'll peer. It takes a little

Verse

time you know, to check back one whole year! 3., 6. When Santa Claus gets your letter, I really do believe, you'll head his list, you

1.
won't be missed by Santa on Christmas Eve.

2.
4. When Eve.

When Christmas Morn Is Dawning

Traditional Swedish

Strum Pattern: 4
Pick Pattern: 3

Verse
Moderately Slow

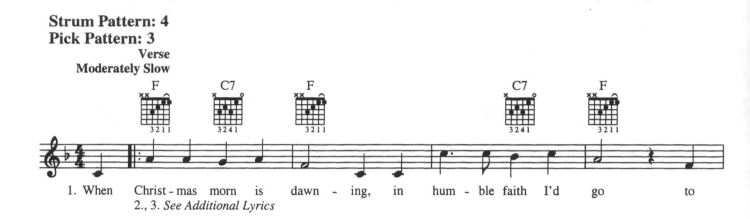

1. When Christ-mas morn is dawn-ing, in hum-ble faith I'd go to
2., 3. *See Additional Lyrics*

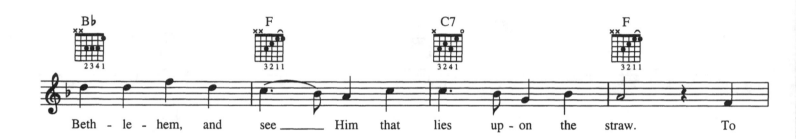

Beth - le - hem, and see _____ Him that lies up - on the straw. To

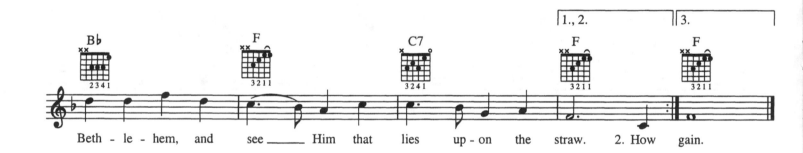

Beth - le - hem, and see _____ Him that lies up - on the straw. 2. How gain.

Additional Lyrics

2. How good of You, my Savior,
To come from Heav'n above!
O take away my sinning.
Protect me with Thy love.

3. Blest Jesus, how I need Thee,
The children's dearest friend!
O may I never grieve Thee
With pain of sin again.

You Make It Feel Like Christmas

Words and Music by Neil Diamond

Strum Pattern: 4
Pick Pattern: 3

Verse
Slowly

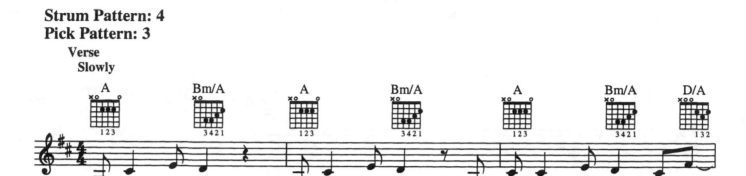

1. Look at   us   now.   Part of   it   all.   In   spite of   it   all,   we're still __
2. Lov - ers   in love.   Just like   we were.   Be - ing   a - part's   a   lone -

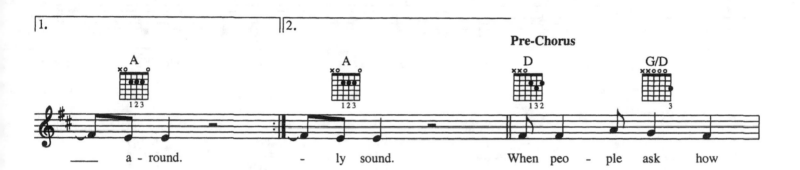

1.
___ a - round.

2.   Pre-Chorus
- ly sound.   When peo - ple   ask   how

we stay to - geth - er,   I   say   you nev - er   let ___   me down.   And

Chorus

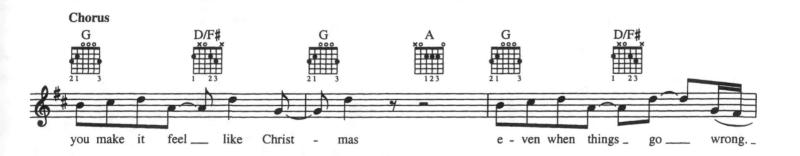

you make it   feel __ like Christ - mas   e - ven when things __ go __ wrong. __

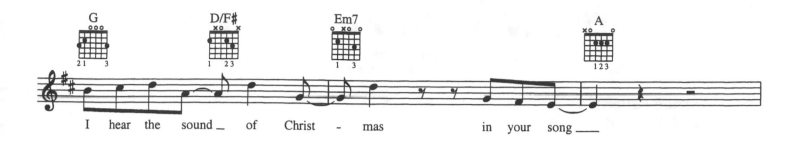

I hear the sound of Christ - mas in your song ___

To Coda ⊕

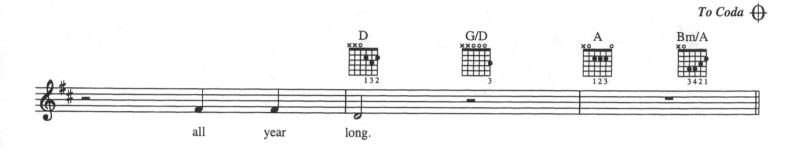

all year long.

Verse

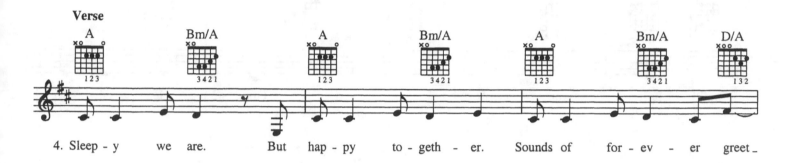

4. Sleep - y we are. But hap - py to - geth - er. Sounds of for - ev - er greet ___

Pre-Chorus

___ the day. So wake up the kids. Put on some tea.

D.S. al Coda   ⊕ Coda

Light up the tree; it's Christ - mas day. Yeah.   All year

long.   Light up the tree; it's Christ - mas time.

The White World of Winter

Words by Mitchell Parish
Music by Hoagy Carmichael

Strum Pattern: 4
Pick Pattern: 3

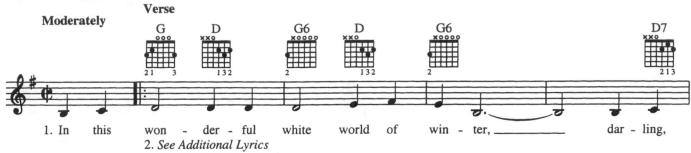

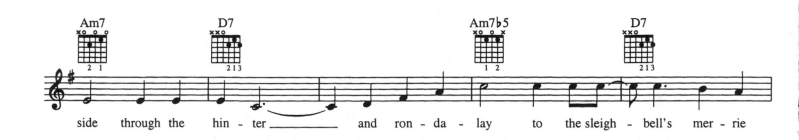

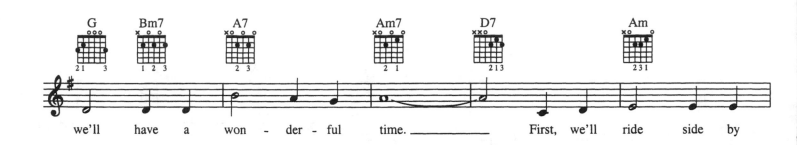

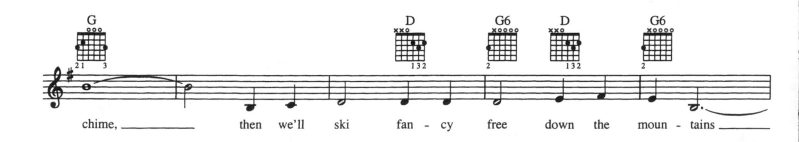

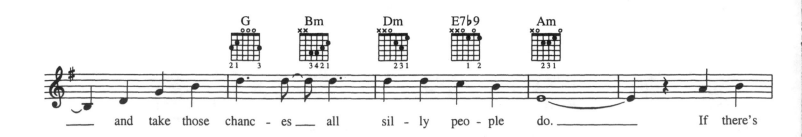

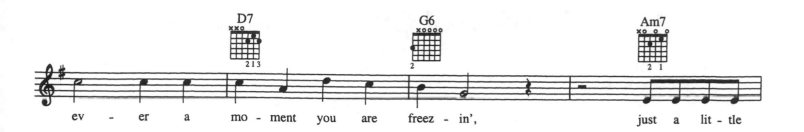

ev – er a mo – ment you are freez – in', just a lit – tle

squeez – in' could be might – y pleas – in'. In this

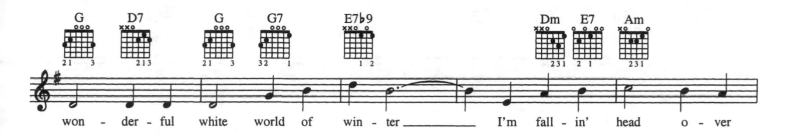

won – der – ful white world of win – ter _____ I'm fall – in' head o – ver

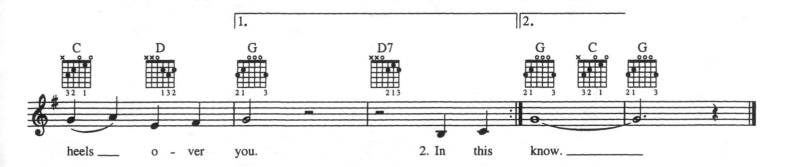

| 1. | 2. |

heels ___ o – ver you. 2. In this know. _____

Additional Lyrics

2. In this wonderful white world of winter,
Darling, we'll have a wonderful time;
If we prayed it would snow all this winter
I ask ya, is that a terr'ble, horr'ble crime?
I can't wait till we skate on Lake Happy
And sup a hot buttered cup in the afterglow.
If there's ever a moment you're not laughin',
Maybe a toboggan; split your little noggin'.
In this wonderful white world of winter,
I'm thinkin' you are the sweetest one I know.

Wonderful Christmastime

Words and Music by McCartney

Strum Pattern: 2
Pick Pattern: 4

Verse
Brightly

1. The mood is right, ___ the spir-it's up, ___
2., 3. *See Additional Lyrics*

we're here to-night ___ and that's e-nough. ___

Chorus

Sim - ply hav - ing a won - der - ful Christ - mas - time.

Sim - ply hav - ing a won - der - ful Christ - mas - time. time.

Bridge

The choir of chil - dren sing their song. (They prac - tised

all year long.) Ding dong, ding dong. Ding dong, ding.

D.C. al Coda

Repeat & Fade

Additional Lyrics

2. The party's on,
   The feeling's here
   That only comes
   This time of year.

3. The word is out
   About the town,
   To lift a glass.
   Oh, don't look down.

271

Your Favorite Music For Guitar Made Easy

American Folksongs for Easy Guitar

Over 70 songs, including: All The Pretty Little Horses • Animal Fair • Aura Lee • Billy Boy • Buffalo Gals (Won't You Come Out Tonight) • Bury Me Not On The Lone Prairie • Camptown Races • (Oh, My Darling) Clementine • (I Wish I Was In) Dixie • The Drunken Sailor • Franky And Johnny • Home On The Range • Hush, Little Baby • I've Been Working On The Railroad • Jacob's Ladder • John Henry • My Old Kentucky Home • She'll Be Comin' Round The Mountain • Shenandoah • Simple Gifts • Swing Low, Sweet Chariot • The Wabash Cannon Ball • When Johnny Comes Marching Home • and more!
00702031 ....$12.95

The Big Christmas Collection

Includes over 70 Christmas favorites, such as: Ave Maria • Blue Christmas • Deck the Hall • Feliz Navidad • Frosty the Snow Man • Happy Holiday • A Holly Jolly Christmas • Joy to the World • O Holy Night • Silver and Gold • Suzy Snowflake • You're All I Want for Christmas • and more.
00698978...................................$16.95

The Broadway Book

93 unforgettable songs from 57 shows, including: Ain't Misbehavin' • Beauty and the Beast • Cabaret • Camelot • Don't Cry for Me Argentina • Edelweiss • Hello Dolly • I Whistle a Happy Tune • One • People • Sound of Music • Tomorrow • and more.
00702015 ...$17.95

The Big Book of Children's Songs

A comprehensive collection of 88 songs, including: Alphabet Song • Baa Baa Black Sheep • The Ballad of Davy Crockett • Beauty and the Beast • Bingo • The Brady Bunch • The Candy Man • Edelweiss • Everything Is Beautiful • (Meet) The Flintstones • I'm Popeye the Sailor Man • On Top of Spaghetti • Puff the Magic Dragon • Sailing Sailing • Supercalifragilisticexpialidocious • Twinkle, Twinkle Little Star • Yellow Submarine • and more.
00702027 ....$9.95

The Classic Country Book

Over 100 favorite country hits including: Another Somebody Done Somebody Wrong Song • Could I Have This Dance • Don't It Make My Brown Eyes Blue • Elvira • Folsom Prison Blues • The Gambler • Heartaches By The Number • I Fall To Pieces • Kiss An Angel Good Mornin' • Lucille • The Most Beautiful Girl In The World • Oh, Lonesome Me • Rocky Top • Sixteen Tons • Tumbling Tumbleweeds • Will The Circle Be Unbroken • You Needed Me • and more.
00702018...................................$19.95

The Classic Rock Book

89 monumental songs from the '60's, '70's and '80's, such as: American Woman • Born To Be Wild • Cocaine • Dust In The Wind • Fly Like An Eagle • Gimme Three Steps • I Can See For Miles • Layla • Magic Carpet Ride • Reelin' In The Years • Sweet Home Alabama • Tumbling Dice • Walk This Way • You Really Got Me • and more.
00698977...................................$19.95

National Anthems For Easy Guitar

50 official national anthems in their original language, complete with strum and pick patterns and chord frames. Countries represented include Australia, Brazil, Canada, Cuba, France, Germany, Great Britain, Haiti, Irish Republic, Mexico, Peru, Poland, Russia, Sweden, United States of America, and more.
00702025 ....$12.95

The New Country Hits Book

100 hot country hits including: Achy Breaky Heart • Ain't Going Down ('Til The Sun Comes Up) • Blame It On Your Heart • Boot Scootin' Boogie • Chattahoochee • Don't Rock The Jukebox • Friends In Low Places • Honky Tonk Attitude • I Feel Lucky • I Take My Chances • Little Less Talk And A Lot More Action • Mercury Blues • One More Last Chance • Somewhere In My Broken Heart • T-R-O-U-B-L-E • The Whiskey Ain't Workin' • and more.
00702017...................................$19.95

FOR MORE INFORMATION, SEE YOUR LOCAL MUSIC DEALER, OR WRITE TO:

HAL•LEONARD® CORPORATION
7777 W. BLUEMOUND RD. P.O. BOX 13819 MILWAUKEE, WI 53213

Contact Hal Leonard on the internet at http://www.halleonard.com